SNAILBEACH LEAD MINE, SHROPSHIRE

Shropshire Mines Trust

Edited by
Adrian Pearce

First published by Peter Burgess 2008

© Copyright Shropshire Mines Trust Ltd, 2008

Front cover illustration: by I.A. Cooper

Back cover: A selection of minerals from Snailbeach Lead Mine
(Nick Southwick Collection)

ISBN 978-0-9556081-2-4

Preface

The Shropshire Mines Trust Ltd and Shropshire Caving & Mining Club have been visiting Snailbeach Mine for many years. They have taken a vast number of visitors around the surface and underground and, over the last few years, opened the mine on National Heritage Day to hundreds more visitors every year. During this time they have often been asked if there is a book that tells the history of the mine in simple terms.

We have finally got around to producing such a book and we hope this will answer all of the questions you may have about this fantastic site. Some of the mining terms used may be unfamiliar to you and these are described in a glossary at the end of the book. It is always difficult to decide whether to give distances and weights in imperial, metric or both but, since the mine was driven using imperial measurements, these have been used in the text if referring to old workings. If you are not familiar with these then 1 foot = 0.3 metres, 1 yard = 3 feet, 1 fathom = 6 feet and 1 pound = 0.45 kilograms. The symbol commonly used for inches is ", eg 60". Money was in pounds, shillings and pence, where there were 12 pennies in a shilling and 20 shillings in a pound.

We have purposely designed this book to be read by someone with only a general interest. If you want to know more, there is a bibliography pointing you to more detailed descriptions of the mine, etc.

Snailbeach Mine has the best set of preserved lead mine buildings and features in Shropshire and probably the whole country. As well as being a fascinating place to walk around, it is a valuable historical resource for schools or other groups. Most of the site is owned by Shropshire County Council and managed by Shropshire Mines Trust Ltd. The latter organisation can arrange surface and underground organised tours if required. There is a visit co-ordinator and details can be found on the website for the mine :-

http://www.snailbeachmine.org.uk

Acknowledgements

This book was a joint effort from the following people :-

David Adams	Eileen Bowen	Andy Browning
Ian Cooper	Andy Cuckson	Pam Curley
John Davies	Steve Holding	Kelvin Lake
Georgia Lloyd	Ken Lock	Mike Moore
Adrian Pearce	David Poyner	Michael Shaw
Peter Sheldrake	Nick Southwick	Mike Worsfold

In addition, thanks must go to many other members of the Shropshire Mines Trust Ltd and Shropshire Caving & Mining Club who have devoted so much time to exploration, preservation and research of Snailbeach Mine. Also to the people who live in the villages of Snailbeach and Stiperstones, of whom many are descended from the miners and are justifiably proud of the site. Finally in memory of the late Malcolm Newton, whose drawings inspired many people to visit the mines.

The Editor operating a BEV underground battery loco as part of the Trust's mining display *(A.J. Pearce)*

Contents

Preface 3
Acknowledgements 4
Introduction 6
Geology 11
History 16
Working Conditions 51
George's Shaft Disaster 66
Living Conditions 76
Surface Tour 93
Underground Tour 119
Snailbeach District Railway 140
Wildlife 151
Bibliography 158
Glossary of Terms 165
Shropshire Mines Trust Ltd 170
Shropshire Caving & Mining Club 172

Introduction

A few miles south-west of Shrewsbury lies a range of hills called the Stiperstones. These are geologically very old and there is much superstition surrounding them. One rock feature is called the Devil's Chair and, when mist obscures it, the Devil is said to have come down to sit in it - or so the drinkers in the Stiperstones Inn maintain! Anyone sitting in his chair today, and looking west, will see a peaceful scene of green fields and farms. It is hard to believe but this pleasant rural scenery was once the site of a thriving mining industry, which extracted lead, zinc, barite and other minerals. In 1875, this small area produced over 10% of the UK lead ore and up to the First World War produced about 25% of UK barite.

At that time there would have been huge spoil heaps and smoke from chimneys, as powerful steam engines pumped water out of the many lead mines on the land below. Amongst these, Snailbeach Mine (2 miles south of Minsterley at NGR SJ375022) was the biggest lead mine in Shropshire and at one time it is reputed to have yielded the greatest volume of lead per acre of any mine in Europe. The underground working area extended ¾ mile east-west and about 250 yards north-south, working down to the 552 yard level, and covered a surface area of approximately 77 acres. Underground mining ceased here in 1955 but the surface buildings are the most complete set in the district and probably the country. Although the miners mainly extracted lead ore (galena), smaller quantities of barite, calcite, fluorspar, silver, zinc and witherite were also obtained.

To many older people, mention mining and they immediately think of coal. They retain memories of tall headgears, chimneys belching smoke, huge spoil tips and everything covered in coal dust, including the surrounding houses. Although metalliferous mines also had the engines and machinery, they tended to be a lot cleaner. Many villages and towns in Shropshire grew up around new mines and became wealthy as the mines prospered. The village of Snailbeach is a typical example where houses and

The Stiperstones range of hills in South Shropshire, looking north towards Shrewsbury. A peaceful rural scene to modern visitors. *(D.A.Mortimer)*

Spring lambs on the Stiperstones. *(D.A.Mortimer)*

mine are closely intermingled. When admiring the buildings and the sheer scale of the workings, however, don't forget the skill and perseverance of the people that made all this possible. The miner drilling at a rock face hundreds of feet underground; the engine driver tending his machinery with loving care; women and children on the surface in all weathers crushing and preparing the ore for smelting; masons who built the engine houses; carpenters who made the headgears; smelters who converted the ore into saleable metal and many others.

It was not only these who depended on the mine for their livelihood; there were the local shopkeepers, farmers, blacksmiths, carpenters, builders and especially innkeepers! For the larger mines there were shareholders relying on dividends, often retired people hoping for a bonanza to supplement their income. The landowners received rent and royalties and many families made their wealth from mines. Some of these were absentee landowners such as the Marquis of Bath and Earl of Tankerville. All drew an income from the mines and it was a catastrophe for a community when a mine closed. In some places, the miners and their families moved elsewhere to find work and left ghost towns behind which rapidly became piles of stones. Today we have no working mines left in Shropshire and, except to the trained eye, most of the mine sites are now no more than humps and bumps in the landscape. The one major exception is Snailbeach Mine, which can justifiably claim to have the best set of preserved lead mine buildings in Britain.

This book does not claim to be the definitive history of Snailbeach Mine. It is aimed at the general public who have had their curiosity aroused by the headgear and buildings and wish to know a bit more. It will attempt to give you an insight into what was there and who the people were who made it work. It must be stressed that, although much of the site is on public-owned land, some parts are private. Where this is the case, you should always ask permission before visiting them. Remember that a mine site can still be dangerous, so make sure that neither yourself nor children under your control climb on old buildings or machinery. You should never explore mine workings unless you are properly equipped and experienced.

The Snailbeach mine site today, with its fascinating mix of woodland, mining remains and houses. *(Kelvin Lake - I.A.Recordings)*

View of Snailbeach about 1900, with steam and smoke coming from the chimneys and engines of the mine. Around the site can be seen several houses, some of which survive and are still lived in today. *(K.C.Lock)*

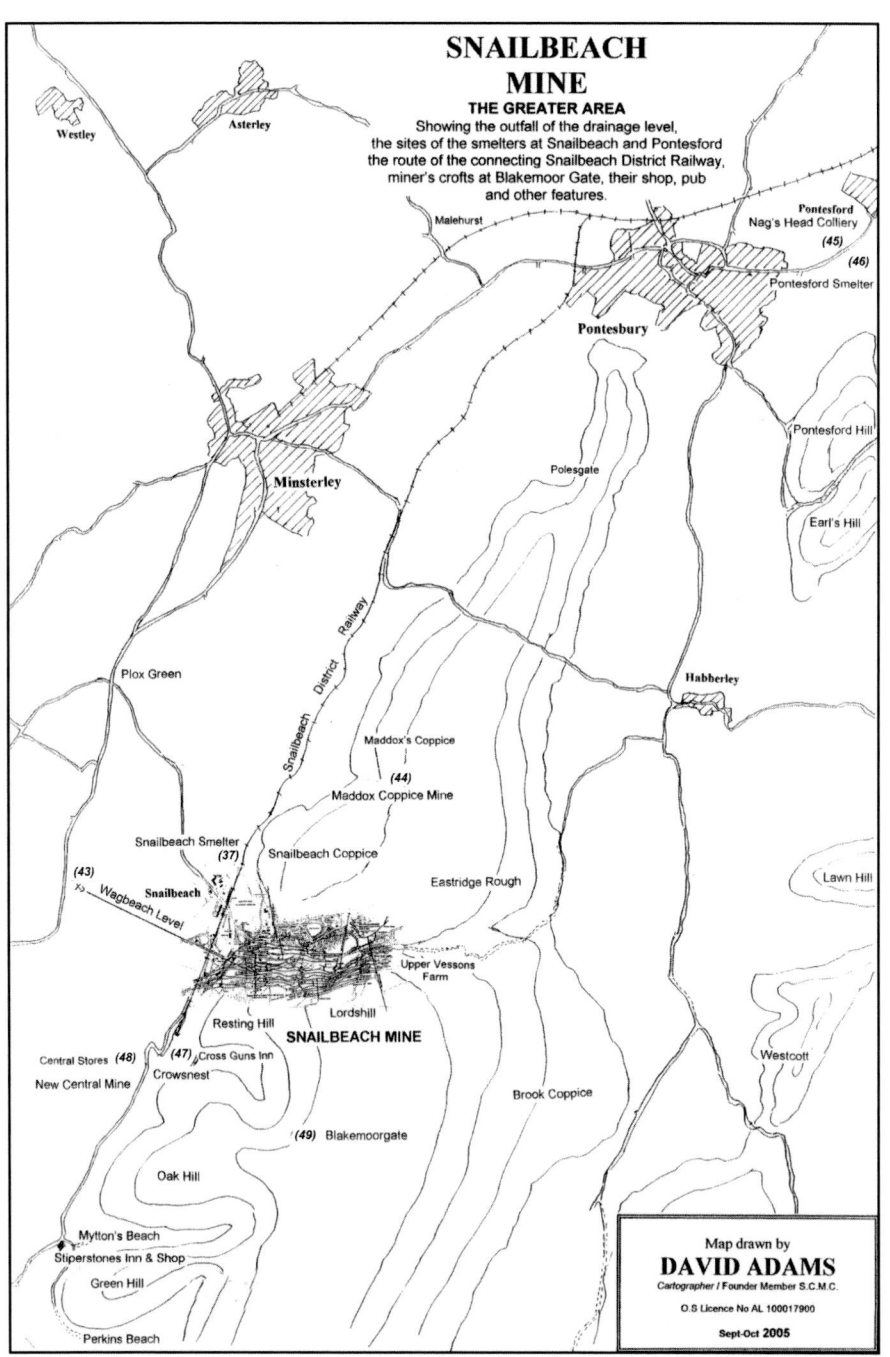

General location map of Snailbeach mine. Numbers in brackets refer to features and sites mentioned in the "Surface Tour" section. *(David Adams)*

Geology

The main rocks in which the minerals have been deposited at the Snailbeach Mine are called Mytton Flags. These are grit/shale sedimentary rocks laid down in the early Ordovician times, approximately 450 million years ago, and now make up most of the rock types that lie at the base of the Stiperstones range of hills.

The Mytton Flags consist of fine silts and grits deposited onto the beds of ancient estuaries from rivers eroding away even more ancient mountains. These sediments built up in layers and now attain a present day thickness of over 2,000ft.

As geological time progressed, these sediments were subject to major earth movements causing them to fold and fault. At a later stage, there was deep seated igneous activity, possibly in the Devonian period approximately 380 million years ago. Super-heated brine waters, containing dissolved chemical elements, ascended from the igneous mass and found their way along the faults. In doing so, they slowly cooled and released minerals which filled the voids of the faults and became the mineral veins that we know today.

Minerals were deposited at different cooling temperatures within the faults, barite, witherite and calcite in the upper parts of the veins, galena, calcite and quartz deeper, and still deeper the minerals sphalerite, calcite and quartz. In theory, copper and tin minerals should be found at depth but this has never been proven.

You can see good surface exposures of the Mytton Flags at three locations :-

- side of the old railway line, close to Crows Nest Dingle (NGR SJ370018)
- right side of the lane leading up to the Lords Hill Chapel (NGR SJ 378022)
- behind the bungalow to the left of the Stiperstones Inn (NGR SJ363005).

All of these exposures can be seen to dip at approximately 50 degrees due to ancient earth movements.

The other rock type encountered underground at the Snailbeach Mine is Stiperstones Quartzite. This is very hard rock, consisting of almost pure fine silica sand laid down in the shallow tropical seas of the early Ordovician period. However, although these rocks have been subjected to folding and faulting in a similar way to the Mytton Flags, for some reason they never laid themselves open to mineral deposition. They almost acted as a cap rock, halting migrating mineral fluids from the Mytton Flags. This was found to be the case, and to the great disappointment of the mine owners, when they drove levels in an easterly direction from Chapel Shaft and met with the Stiperstones Quartzite at the 112 Yard Level and below.

Today the Stiperstones Quartzite can easily be recognised on the surface, it is the rock that makes up the famous Stiperstones Ridge which includes The Devil's Chair, Cranberry Rock and Nipstone Rock.

The minerals found in the veins at Snailbeach Mine are :-

Common
Barite - barium sulphate ($BaSO_4$)
Calcite - calcium carbonate ($CaCO_3$)
Galena - lead sulphide (PbS_2)
Iron Pyrites - iron sulphide (FeS)
Quartz - silicon dioxide (SiO_2)
Sphalerite - zinc sulphide (ZnS)
Witherite - barium carbonate ($BaCO_3$)

Rare
Cerussite - lead carbonate ($PbCO_3$)
Chalcopyrite – copper/iron sulphide ($CuFeS_2$)
Pyromorphite - chloro-phosphate of lead ($3Pb_3P_2O_8.PbCl_2$)

Recorded but not seen
Fluorspar - calcium fluoride (CaF_2)

'Spar Box' decorated with minerals donated by the late Emily Griffiths
(Shropshire Mines Trust)

Galena, Lead Sulphide (PbS)

Pyromorphite, Chloro-Phosphate of Lead $(3Pb_3P_2O_8.PbCl_2)$ - rare

Barite, Barium Sulphate $((BaSO_4)$

Witherite, Barium Carbonate $(BaCO_3)$

Quartz, Silicon Dioxide (SiO_2)

Chalcopyrite, Copper/Iron Sulphide $(CuFeS_2)$ – rare

See back cover for colour versions of these pictures

All minerals from the "Nick Southwick Collection"

Sphalerite, Zinc Sulphide (ZnS)

Iron Pyrites, Iron Sulphide (FeS_2)

Calcite, Calcium Carbonate ($CaCO_3$)

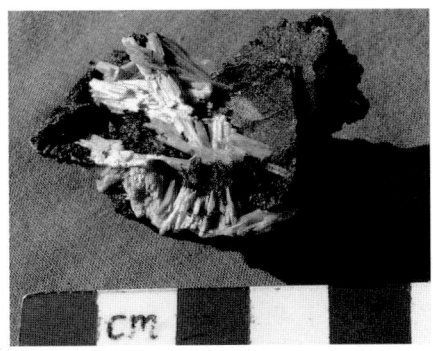
Cerussite, Lead Carbonate ($PbCO_3$)
- rare

*All minerals from the
"Nick Southwick Collection"*

Fluorspar, Calcium Fluoride (CaF_2)

History

The Roman Era – 1500

It is believed that the Romans were the first to exploit lead in Shropshire and that they mined some of it at Snailbeach. They did this by means of open trenches and shallow levels and shafts. An ingot (called a pig) of lead from that period was found at Snailbeach in 1796 and has the equivalent of over 2 ounces of silver per ton of lead, one of the reasons that the Romans were so interested in mining this metal. According to reports from the middle of the 19th Century, the Roman workings were still clearly visible at Snailbeach at that time and the miners referred to the upper level as the Roman Level. All such remains, however, have unfortunately been destroyed by later periods of working.

A small number of Roman lead pigs (ingots) have been found locally, ie

1) Weight 190lbs, dated AD117-138, found 1767, probably 3 miles NW of Bishops Castle. Now at Linley Hall.

2) Weight 193lbs, dated AD117-138, measuring 22" x 7", found 1796 at Snailbeach Farm (this is the old Snailbeach Farm which is the half-timbered house behind the large grassed-over hillocks). Now at British Museum.

3) No details and has not been seen since 1827,

4) Weight 185lbs, dated AD117-128, found 1851 at the Roveries Snead, ¾ mile NE of church and 1 mile W of Linley Hall. Was at Liverpool Museum but now believed lost.

5) Weight 173lbs, AD117-138, found in 1851 near to where (2) was found earlier. There is no record of it so it may be confused with the original find.

6) A lead pig was apparently found in the open workings at Roman Gravels but nothing further is known about this.

Most of the pigs found in Shropshire bear the inscription IMP HADRIANI AVG (Emperor Hadrian ruled from 117-138AD). 144 English pounds are the equivalent of 200 Roman pounds and this may be the weight that the Roman lead manufacturers were aiming at in producing the Shropshire lead ingots.

Replica of the Roman lead ingot found in 1767, made by the Shropshire Mines Trust Ltd in 2003, it weighs 190lbs and was based on the one held at Linley Hall. *(Kelvin Lake - I.A.Recordings)*

Detail of the inscription on the SMT replica. Most of the Roman ingots found in Shropshire bear the inscription "IMP HADRIANI AVG.".
(Kelvin Lake - I.A.Recordings)

Mining methods would have changed very little in the centuries after the Romans left and workings would have continued to be shallow and drained by levels driven from the valley sides. Lead continued to be a valuable commodity and, although there is no mention in the Domesday Book of lead mining in

Shropshire, there are some early references to mining in this area. Following the Norman conquest, the area was designated as a royal forest called 'Tenfrenstanes', from which the name Stiperstones is derived. Towards the end of the 12th Century, this was under the care of Baron Peter Corbet of Caus Castle but he seems to have upset King Henry II at some stage. It is recorded that the King 'engrossed' the whole or a great part of, the profits of the Shelve mines, owing to Corbet, baron of Caus Castle, being in disgrace".

It cannot be said for certain whether there was any mining at Snailbeach during this time. Shelve was obviously an important lead mining centre for the area and the mines referred to could have been the nearby Grit or Roman Gravel Mines, which are equally as old. However, it would seem logical to assume that anywhere that had previously been mined for lead would continue to be so. Control of mining in the area was delegated to an official called a 'Justice of the Forest', to whom payment was made for a lease to work the mines. The Justice would then pass this money over to the Sheriff of Shropshire who accounted for it to the King. Mining in the area was obviously an important income for the King and he took this as either money or lead itself, depending on his needs at the time. Lead for the King always seems to have been sent to Gloucester first and it would have been transported by boat along the River Severn from Shrewsbury. The following records from the time give an idea of what was happening and some of the lead may have originated at Snailbeach :-

1179   Thomas Fitz-Bernard, a Justice of the Forest, leased the lead mine at Shelfe to one Nicholas Poncler for one year at a rent of £55, to be paid by even installments at Easter and Michaelmas following. The Justice paid this over to Hugh Pantulf, Sheriff of Shropshire, who delivered it in full to the King the following year upon receiving an order to do so.

1180   Thomas Fitz-Bernard let mines for 40 Marks (£26.13s.4d) and paid this to Hugh Pantulf. The latter accounted for forwarding 60 cart loads of lead worth £21, for the King's use. Also 120 cart loads of lead to Gloucester by the King's order. After deducting transportation costs, he paid a balance of 6d into the Treasury and was quit.

1182 Hugh Pantulf forwarded lead worth £389 from Shrewsbury to Gloucester, as certified by witnesses. The latter process is possibly because of the extremely large value of the consignment, indicating that the mines must have been very productive at that time.

1182 Hugh Pantulf purchased 110 cart loads of other lead for the King costing £38.10s.0d. This was sent to the convent of Amesbury in Wiltshire, which had been dissolved in 1177 on the grounds of immorality! The lead helped to re-roof the buildings which were re-colonised by a 'purer sisterhood'.

Lead continued to be forwarded to Gloucester by the Sheriff, ie

DATE	AMOUNT	VALUE	TRANSPORT COSTS
1183	30 cart loads	£10.10s.0d.	£18s.9d.
1184	not known	£4.11s.0d	£8s.3½d.
1185	30 cart loads	not known	£1.8s.9d
1185	30 cart loads	not known	£2.6s.3d

Of the two consignments in 1185 as above, the first was sent from Shrewsbury (on the River Severn) and the second direct from the mines. The reason for the latter is not known as it obviously cost more to transport it overland. Perhaps there was an urgent need for it and the King could not wait.

1220 Robert Corbet paid tithes to Shrewsbury Abbey of his share of the produce of the Shelve mines. Tithes were a religious tax and this only seems to have been a temporary measure since his descendant Thomas was no longer doing this in

	1270. Thus the fitting out of Shrewsbury Abbey was partly financed by local lead mines.
1278	3 wagon loads of lead were sent from Shelve to Builth Castle.

1500 – 1800

1552	John Clifton held a mine in Hogstow Forest, which was possibly Snailbeach.
1676-1686	some Derbyshire miners held leases at Snailbeach. Ancient crude smelters called boles were found on top of the Stiperstones according to 'The Miner's Dictionary" by William Hooson in 1747, "There are places where we may suppose that the Lead-Ore has been carried several Miles, for the conveniency of air, to a fit Place, because we see no Mines to have ever been near them; but above all, upon the Hills, called Stiperstones in Shropshire, they may be found very common, and are very little Places, and they seem to have done their Business by laying a round Row of Stones on the Ground, and placing the Fire in the middle; they picked the Ore on, or near the Surface of the Ground on those Hills, and perhaps melted not one hundred Weight in one Place."
	It is thus likely that early smelting of Snailbeach lead ore was done in boles on the adjacent Stiperstones hills. At the time of writing, a survey of possible smelting bole sites on the Stiperstones is being carried out but, as yet, it is not possible to identify any that were associated with Snailbeach.
1761-1766	the site was leased by Thomas Powys who sunk a series of shafts.
1766-1772	a new partnership took over the mine and produced 505 tons of lead ore, which is quite appreciable for a small scale operation.

| 1782 | Thomas Lovett of Chirk took a 21 year lease which encompassed "…all and every the mines of lead and lead ore, copper and copper ore, black jack and calamine and all manner of mines and veins and seams of coal which should or might be found, opened or discovered in, upon or under the banks, lands and grounds belonging to the said Viscount Weymouth in the Manor of Minsterley" |

The following year, Lovett formed the "Snailbeach Company" with nine others and this produced the capital necessary for larger scale working of the mine. There were 16 shares and the partners were :-

- Thomas Lovett of Chirk, Denbighshire   2½ shares
- Thomas Smith of Minera, Denbighshire   2 shares
- Thomas Price of Oxford Coffee House, London   1½ shares
- Randle Jones of Penylan, Denbighshire   2 shares
- Richard Salisbury of Oswestry, Salop   2 shares
- Jeffrey Williams of Chirk, Denbighshire   2 shares
- John Lloyd of Hafodynos, Denbighshire   1 share
- John Lovett of Oswestry, Salop   1 share
- Ellis Jones of Llanyplodwyl, Salop   1 share
- William Lovett of Chirk, Denbighshire   1 share

An Inventory of Snailbeach Lead Mines

		£	s	d
7 Horses	Surly	5	0	0
	Jett	2	12	0
	Bosse	4	0	0
	Dolle	5	5	0
	Jewell	6	6	0
	Great Lyon and little Lyon	5	5	0
A Ginn		5	0	0
4 new Ginn baskits		2	0	0
2 old ones		0	5	0
2 Turne Barrels and Two pair of Stows		0	10	0
A new Capsey Rope		9	0	0
3 Bays of new building		35	0	0
A Smale Capsey Rope		2	10	0
A Enjine		140	0	0
A Smith Shap 2 Budle Hours and bing		10	0	0
4 Drawing baskits		0	10	0
A Chest		0	12	0
Five Tons of Waste		15	0	0
A Beame and Skales		0	10	0
Three Buckets		0	2	0
Two Hammers		0	3	0
One Calera he		0	1	0
One Sive		0	5	0
Two Shovels		0	3	4
Six Corves		0	9	0
One Wheale Barrow		0	5	0
Railes boards and Slobs at Sawpitt		2	10	0
A Wagon		1	1	0
8 Shovels		0	13	4
Miners Tools	400 watt	5	0	0
Ballance Due to Snailbeach Co. at Ladyday 1770. at Xmass 1769		91	16	0½

Copy of the Inventory of 'Snailbeach Lead Mines' in 1769. Amongst the items, it lists 'Ginn' with 4 new baskets and 2 old ones, 3 bays of new building, plus 'A Engine'.

In 1784, Thomas Lovett's company leased land along the road between Pontesford and Pontesbury and sank shafts to start the Nag's Head Colliery, mainly for smelting but later also to provide coal for the boilers of engines working at Snailbeach Mine. At the same time, they built a smelter opposite the colliery in Pontesford to process the lead ore. This was then used to smelt all of the ore from Snailbeach, which would have been transported there in carts. There were many complaints about the poisonous fumes coming from the works and it was not until 1832 that they built two chimneys (150ft and 180ft) to try to take away the fumes from the village. There was a 360ft long horizontal flue from the works to the chimneys, which were themselves of substantial structure. One of the chimneys had a 28ft internal diameter at the base. There is an interesting description of the works by John Wood Warter writing in 1862.

"Those who visit the lead district must not omit to visit these smelting furnaces for, however deleterious the fumes thrown off may be, and however one shrinks from the pale cadaverous faces of the smelters with pity and sorrow, one may ease the labour of the day with a small 'douceur' and some kind words, which will not be thrown away. The damage to the health of the men done by the smelting houses is mentioned in the 'Additions to Camden'. The ore is run into 'pieces' either in smelting houses or cupolas. The latter were introduced nearly 50 years ago and are considered as less prejudicial to the health of the workman than the former. The smoke of the lead produces palsies, consumption, the 'byon' which resembles the quinsy and a disorder of the bowels called the 'belland'. In the days of my boyhood, this was the case at Pontesford, and indeed, till the great smelting chimneys were erected, nor is the evil entirely done away with, though it be nothing like that occasioned by the fumes of sulphur at Swansea thrown off by the copper smelting. Formerly at Pontesford smelting houses, great quantities of oil were drunk by the smelters to counteract the evil effects of arsenic. In examining the works last year, I was told that oil is still used, but not so much. Years ago, many experiments were tried on the smoke as it issued from the chimneys by a well known practitioner in the neighbourhood.

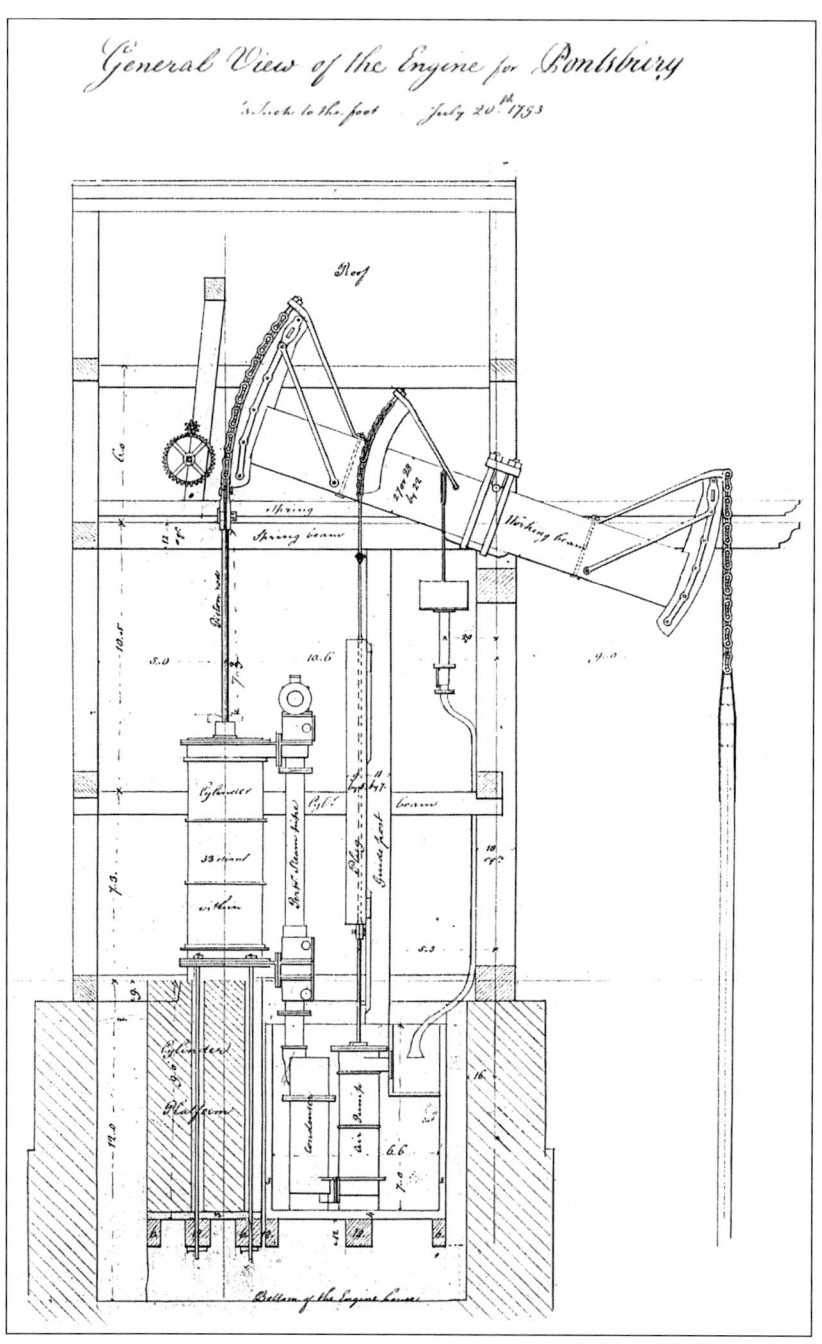

Sketch of the 1793 Pontesbury steam engine based on a drawing in the Boulton & Watt Collection.

Pontesford Colliery pumping engine house. When the mine closed, before the 1840s, the building was converted into a house, and is still lived in today. (K.C.Lock)

Among other things it was observed that no bird could pass through the volume unscathed, but fell down dead.."

The workers also had other remedies to counteract the effect of the fumes, including oatmeal water with sulphuric acid, Epsom salts or lozenges containing sulphur, sugar, peppermint and sodium sulphide. Of equal concern to neighbours was the effect of lead fumes on cattle. The lead particles in the fumes would coat grass and be ingested by the animals, leading to death by lead poisoning known as bellanding.

At the main site, the company sank Old Shaft (later called George's Shaft after the engine driver) around 1797 and this eventually reached a depth of 750ft. The depths of all subsequent underground workings are measured in yards below this shaft collar, eg the 40 Yard Level is 120ft below this point but not necessarily that depth elsewhere below surface. Winding would have been by a horse gin (gin being an old word for engine), using a rope wound around the spindle so that both ends hung down the shaft and were attached to kibbles (large metal buckets). One kibble would be at the bottom of the shaft while the other was at the top and they passed half way. A 1,200 yard long drainage tunnel known as Wagbeach Adit was driven from the bottom of the Hope Valley and this intersected the workings at the 112 Yard level, thereby draining the mine to that depth. By 1793, a beam engine had been installed to pump water up George's Shaft to the drainage level and, by 1797, the mine was 540ft deep. Workings 'below adit' had to be kept dry by pumping the water up to the adit to flow out.

1800-1900

Black Tom Shaft was sunk before 1820 and was 120ft deep, ore being wound up with a horse gin. By 1820, the company was obviously doing well as it had paid a total of £43,000 in royalties to the Marquis of Bath, indicating that total sales of lead had been £301,000. In 1827 two reports were prepared, one on the mine and one on the smelt works. The report by Captain Absalom Francis gives some insight into the conditions of the mine at the time. The ore dressing was generally very good, but the initial ore breaking was still by hand using

Site of the waterwheel at the entrance to the Wagbeach Adit. The wheel was on the left and fed with water from the iron sluice above. It operated over a mile of pump rods in the tunnel (lower right) to drain the lower mine workings.

(P.J.Eggleston - I.A.Recordings)

Detail of the sluice gear for the waterwheel at the entrance to the Wagbeach Adit
(P.J.Eggleston - I.A.Recordings)

Inside Wagbeach Adit today. A number of roof falls have blocked the adit and despite efforts by Shropshire Caving & Mining Club to dig through them, this has not yet proved possible
(P.J.Eggleston - I.A.Recordings)

hammers. Francis recommended a "machine worked by horses" that would cost "about £150".

Also in 1827, it was recorded that a new lower adit was being driven from Minsterley to drain the mine to a greater depth. According to the report it was 850 fathoms long and still 1,800 fathoms from the mine. Captain Francis called it the "Calamine Hill Level", although the hill is called the Callow Hill. Captain Francis recommended that work on the adit should be stopped because it would be cheaper to erect a new steam pumping engine than to finish the adit. It was still being driven in the 1870s, although it never did reach the mine. It was probably continued because new lead veins were found in the process, and the ore mined. This often happened when driving adits and was an added bonus.

Captain Francis estimated that the "property at the mine and at the smelting house appears to be worth from £15,000-£20,000" but he was referring to unsold lead. At that time the lead market was in depression and he indicated that the mine should remain profitable, even if selling at the current low price. Exploration could continue and more men might be employed with higher lead prices and a reduction in stock. He went on to say that it was "rich beyond most things I have been acquainted with in mining".

The report on the smelt works by George Henry also sheds light on the conditions there. The fumes from the smelting escaped up a chimney and included a reasonable amount of lead. Henry recommended that a new flue and chimney be installed, which would enable the lead to condense on the walls of the flue to be collected later. Of this he said, "the mass of deposit will amply repay the erection," and also have the great benefit of "doing away with the bad effects of the smoke, and will be a much desirable thing to the neighbourhood." The new flue and condensers were added some years later.

Snailbeach Mine continued to be worked downwards and, by the early 1850s, the workings were over 900ft deep. Engine Shaft (eventually 1,300ft deep) was probably sunk by 1848 and new engines were sited at the surface here, to pump water from

Sketch of a simple horse gin, winding just one kibble (a wood or iron barrel shaped bucket). As shafts got deeper the load was balanced by having 2 ropes and 2 kibbles, one going down as the other came up. *(M. Newton)*

Replica horse-gin, working a single rope and pulley at the former National Mining Museum, Lound Hall.

the deepened workings and to wind ore up the shaft. At the same time, a Day Level was driven to meet this shaft, so that ore could be pushed in trucks straight out of the shaft to the crusher house.

The mineral owner, Marquis of Bath, was an astute businessman and insisted on several covenants as part of the mine lease. These ensured that the partners continually drove exploratory cross cuts and deepened the mine to open up new reserves of lead ore so the mine was never standing idle. One such agreement required the partners to spend "at least £200 per year for the effective carrying on of the mine works with all necessary applications and machinery". The penalty for not doing this was forfeiture of the mine. Another required them "to employ a full complement of miners on sinking engine shaft forty yards below its present bottom and a full complement to drive east and west on the vein for six hundred yards". A further one charged them to spend £2,500 in exploring the ground at Callow Hill to the north of Snailbeach.

The late 1840s and 1850s were the most productive period for the mine, producing over 3,000 tons of lead ore per year. Bagshawe's Directory of 1851 stated that the company paid out salaries of £2,000 per month to a labour force of around 500 persons. In 1857 a new agent, Stephen Eddy, was employed, along with his son James Ray Eddy. They completely refitted the mine and remodelled the dressing floors. A new 60" pumping engine was installed at Engine Shaft to keep pace with the water in the deepened workings. Eddy reduced the work force by 170 and stopped work in the bottom levels, By 1862, however, miners were back extracting ore from the 342 Yard level and preparing the 372 Yard level for development. He introduced an eight hour shift instead of the six hour shift worked at other mines in the area and this caused the miners to go on strike for two weeks. They only resumed work when shown that their wages were higher than at other mines, being paid more for the longer shift.

At Nag's Head Colliery, a second-hand 20" engine was purchased in 1859 for pumping and winding in the shaft, which at that time was 360ft deep. The Snailbeach engineer, Mr Davies, made detailed sketches of the engine parts in his notebook and he must have been quite accomplished as he had to make some of the parts himself in the mine blacksmith's shop. Despite this, he could not tackle all jobs and, when a steam pipe broke, he had to take the fitting to a foundry in Mold to be repaired. Further sketches in the notebook show how an old angle bob was re-used by the Snailbeach Company at their newly opened Malehurst Colliery, to enable them to install pumps in the shaft.

To the east of the property, the sinking of Chapel Shaft was begun by an adjacent landowner, the Earl of Tankerville, who allowed a lease (possibly in 1859) to cash in on the profits being produced by Snailbeach Mine. The Snailbeach Mine Company then took over the lease and began sinking in 1861. By the end of 1861, the shaft was down to the 112 Yard level and in 1862 a small engine house was built to serve the shaft. A second hand steam winch off a ship, referred to as the "marine engine", was used. The shaft reached the 342 Yard level at its deepest. Although there were lead deposits east of Chapel shaft in Tankerville's ground, the continuation of the lead veins was found not to run as far as expected, as the ground was in Stiperstones Quartzite rather than the mineral-bearing Mytton Flags. In the early 1900s, his Lordship demanded unrealistic royalties which forced the company to terminate the lease.

Stephen Eddy died in 1861 and his son took over. In 1862, the Nag's Head Colliery closed and the mine mechanic Vincent Hughes went to take down the engine. This job took 12 days and it was taken to Snailbeach Mine where it was re-conditioned. Up to then, the colliery had produced 27,622 tons of coal but now supplies would be bought from other Shropshire coalfields and delivered by rail. The better quality coal allowed more efficient smelting and Eddy predicted that the savings would more than offset the extra costs. Malehurst Colliery was closed at about the same time. In the same year, the old smelter at Pontesford was abandoned and replaced by a new one nearer to the mine.

Extract from the Snailbeach Mine Day Book for 1862, listing the work carried out by V.Hughes between November 2nd and December 14th. Vincent Hughes was the mine mechanic and is buried by the Chapel on Lords Hill. *(KC.Lock)*

A typical circular buddle. A device for separating finely crushed heavy material, like lead ore, from lighter waste material. *(M. Newton)*

Hand-jigs are another device for separating heavy material from lighter material. By dunking the tray of material in a tub of water the lighter material can be 'washed' away. *(M. Newton)*

Detail of a replica jig, showing the tray with perforated base to allow material to 'wash' through.

The new reverbatory smelter was connected to the mine by a tramway to bring in the lead ore. A brick-arched flue for the fumes ran from the smelt works up the hill to a chimney, which still stands today as a prominent local landmark. The condensed lead fumes were recovered from the flue at regular intervals and estimates of the amount of lead in the flue were always included in the four monthly estimates of stock. For example, 35 tons of lead was estimated to be in the flues in May 1872. At other mines in Britain, arsenic from lead ore also condensed onto the flue walls and was scraped off by young boys who crawled though the flue and packed it into barrels. These were exported to America where the arsenic was used to combat weevils on the cotton crops. However, there is no record of this taking place at Snailbeach.

In 1863, there was a parliamentary enquiry into the condition of mines in Great Britain and it gives a detailed account of the state of Snailbeach Mine at the time.

Chapel Shaft - 340 yards deep, cutting the vein at 280 Yard Level. Used for drawing - done by skips on 1¼" wire ropes.

Engine Shaft - perpendicular to the 282 Yard Level and is continued to the 402 Yard Level following its course and underlaying south 2ft in a fathom [1 in 3]. Winding by 2 kibbles drawn by flat wire ropes 3½" x ⅝". The kibbles pass each other in the vertical section of the shaft.

Old Engine Shaft (Georges Shaft) - down to 252 yards. Used as a footway and occasionally for tools and timber as far as the 150 Yard Level. Below this level it is used as a footway. The ladders are in 10 yard lengths and inclined at 7° to the 150 Yard Level and 10° below that point. The ladders rest on wooden staging [the cages were introduced in 1872]. All the levels are 7ft high and 6ft wide which aids ventilation.

Changing Houses - a row of sheds about 70ft long, 10ft wide, divided into 6 houses. The roofs are very low, no ventilation, floors loose earth. An iron pipe with a fire at one end runs through them all. No provision for washing. [This is not the same as the existing Miners' Dry building].

Dressing Floors - in several places with men and boys being employed.

Snailbeach Miners Benefit Society - this society was managed by a committee annually elected by the miners. The men paid from 4d to 9d per month, depending on their level of pay. If the men were sick or injured they received 7/- per week for 6 months, reducing to 5/6d per week for the next 12 months and after that 4/6d per week. In the case of death, each adult paid 6d and juniors 4d to the funds. The widow received £4. The same sum was paid when the wife of a member died.

Smelting Works - have within the last year been removed from Pontesbury to the mine - since then there has been a good deal of illness amongst the men working in the smelter.

The Inquiry involved questioning of the doctor, mine captain, agent, accountant and a miner and covers a number of topics in varying detail. Below are the more salient points.

Health - long discussion on the health of the miners with indications that Snailbeach was a healthy mine [lead poisoning had not been invented!].

Housing - was described as being mostly mud huts that were anything but healthy. Later described as having 2 rooms and some perhaps 3 (these appear to refer to the number of bedrooms).

The Mine - there is about 2oz of silver per ton. Lowest working level was at 402 yards. Men got 2lbs of tallow candles each per week at a cost of 8d [presumably they had to pay for them]. There was one 60" steam engine for pumping and 4 others. The pumping engine worked about 6 hours per day. There were 6 boilers including "one at the engine we are putting up and one at the lead works".

The Men - not many reside at the mine, the greater proportion are scattered over the hills. There were 203 men working underground and no women worked at the mine. They worked 8 hours per day underground and 12 hours per day if on the surface.

Climbing - 50 minutes to climb up or down 100 fathoms. At a later point a miner said that it took 60 minutes to come up and 30 minutes to go down to the 372 Yard Level. This time was included in the 8 hour working day.

Fatal Accidents - over the past 8 years nobody had been killed from blasting. One man was killed by a falling stone and another fell into a sump.

Blasting - cartridges with straw fuses were used. Iron prickers were used (unusual since copper or bronze did not cause sparks and were safer. The use of iron was common in other mines as well and it proved difficult to make the men change their unsafe habits). Tamping was done with lead ore and carbonate of lime, with brick dust occasionally used.

Extract from the Surveyors Dialing Book for May 2nd 1862, giving details of survey work with a Hedley Dial and Guntens Chain, in Perkins Level, carried out by Jos. Spencer and James Lipton. *(Never on a Sunday Project)*

View across the mine dressing floors, from above Day Level about 1900. On the right is the 1880s compressor house. The rails are coming out of Day Level curving round into the new crusher building. After crushing, the material would drop down to the jigs and buddles on the dressing floor. *(K.C.Lock)*

By 1866, there were 25 partners in the Snailbeach Mining Company and it was decided to dissolve the partnership and create a new limited liability company. This was done by the Snailbeach Mines Estate Act of 1867 and the Snailbeach Mine Company Ltd was formed, although the Lovett family still held the largest amount of shares. The mine manager, James Ray Eddy, resigned in 1870 and was replaced by Henry Dennis. Over the next few years £10,000 was spent on modernising the mine site and a lot of the present day buildings date from that time. The new mechanisation allowed Dennis to reduce the workforce to only 130, with a consequent saving in costs.

A horizontal steam winder was installed on George's Shaft in 1872 and eight new jigging machines and four buddles were erected in a large shed. The winder originally had a double pulley, so that one cage was wound up the shaft whilst the other went down. It was here that the disaster happened in 1895 when the rope broke and 7 men were killed (see separate account). The Snailbeach District Railway to Pontesbury was opened in 1877, to take smelted lead (and later lead ore) to customers. The horse gin on Black Tom Shaft was replaced in the 1880s by a small steam engine, seated on top of its boiler. The crushing engine was reconstructed and, in 1881, a new compressor house and chimney were built, providing power to rock drills and winches underground.

Sectioned view of how the crusher house of the 1870s might have looked. Ore is crushed between iron rollers (held together by the balance weight on the left), it then falls into a revolving screen (trommel), small pieces drop through the screen, while over-sized items fall out the end to be caught by the big wheel and lifted back up for re-crushing. *(M. Newton)*

In later years the ore was wound up in a skip from the 342 Yard level, using a compressed air winch powered from the compressor on surface. It is also believed that the miners used this as an unofficial way up too! However, lead prices began to fall sharply from this time as lead extracted from opencast workings in Spain and Australia could be bought at the docks cheaper than it could be produced from the mines. As a result, in 1884 the company made its first loss of £3,000. The company went into liquidation with the equipment valued at only £2,785. The Marquis of Bath tried to claim £7,000 in compensation for loss of royalties, etc but was persuaded to drop this to only £1,000 on a promise that a new company would continue to work the mine.

The new company (basically Thomas Heaton Lovett, John Jones and Henry Dennis) had to wait until 1885 until it could get possession of the mine and then continued to work the mine on a reduced scale but at a profit. It is interesting that they appear to have reverted to the old style of working with tributers to reduce the cost and risk. In 1887, Thomas Sopwith said that tributers had 19 pitches (working areas) and were paid £10 per ton of lead ore produced. From that was deducted the cost of materials consumed, haulage and dressing at 16/- per ton, smelting at 26/- per ton. This left them with around £4 per ton profit. The company said that lead was selling for £12 per ton and they could not afford to pay them any more. The graph of employee numbers below shows how, at that time, the ratio of surface to underground workers dropped dramatically. Possibly this was because the tributers arranged for their own surface processing and these people were not included as mine employees.

Diagram of the 1881 Compressor house built as part of Henry Dennis's modernisation of the mine. It was used to supply compressed air to underground winches and rock drills. *(M. Newton)*

View from the top of the waste tip by the loco shed of the dressing plant and other machinery around Black Tom Shaft, c1930-40. *(K.C.Lock)*

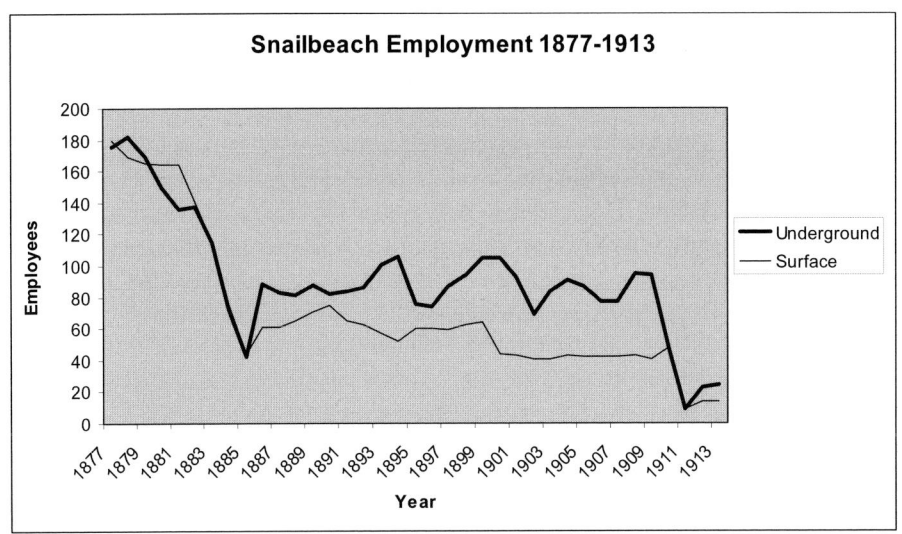

All was not well, however, as lead prices continued to drop and in 1895 the smelter was closed down due to the small output of ore and loss of a major local customer, Burr Bros. of Shrewsbury. From this time onwards, the railway carried lead ore to Pontesbury, instead of smelted lead, so it could be smelted elsewhere. In 1895, the Marquis of Bath had to waive his royalties for three years to enable the company to deepen the mine and open up new reserves of lead ore.

1900-2000

By July 1900, the 552 Yard level was being driven east and west, prior to extracting the lead ore. This was the lowest level reached at Snailbeach, which by then had seen its output fall to only 200 tons in 1905, rising briefly to 1000 tons in 1910. Over the last few years, many local mines had closed due to the rock bottom price for lead but Snailbeach had managed to struggle on as it had particularly rich reserves of lead and it also started mining barite. In the early 20th Century, however, the price dropped so low that even Snailbeach Mine struggled to make a profit. It is likely that the lower workings were abandoned at this time to save on pumping costs. In 1911 the pumping engine was stopped for good and sold as scrap, water flooding the mine up to the 112 Yard level. The Snailbeach Lead Mining Company was liquidated in 1912.

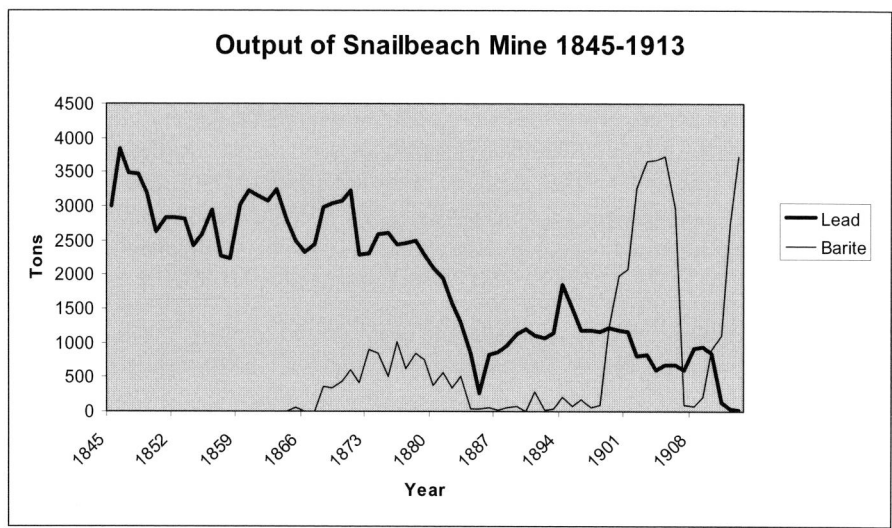

Between 1845-1913, when official returns of output were made, the mine produced a total of

- Lead 131,969 tons
- Barite 42,131 tons
- Zinc 4,384 tons
- Fluorspar 901 tons.

The graph vividly demonstrates the catastrophic drop in lead ore output from 1880 onwards as the price dropped. It recovered temporarily but not for long. At the turn of the century, barite overtook lead as the main product being produced. Zinc is found only at depth so it was only being produced from 1858 onwards and even then not very much was processed. The production of fluorspar is interesting in that it was only produced between 1874-79, possibly it was a one-off deposit. The true total output of the mine may never been known for certain but it is possible that a total of 150,000 tons of lead ore were mined here during the life of the mine.

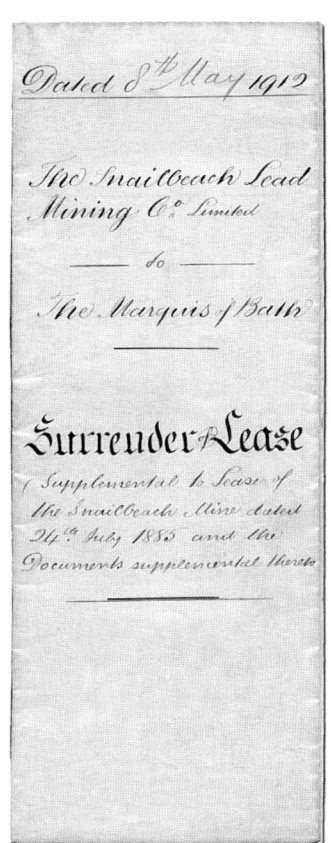

The 8th May, 1912, Agreement between the Marquis of Bath and the Snailbeach Lead Mining Co. surrendering the 31 year lease for the site agreed on 24th July 1885. *(Emily Griffiths Collection)*

Snailbeach Lower Works, c.1910 was a barite processing plant erected in the 1890s. This is now the site of the Village Hall. *(K.C.Lock)*

Black Tom headframe with its twin sheave wheels, in the 1960s. The small wooden engine house can be seen on the left almost hidden by vegetation. *(Shropshire Caving & Mining Club)*

The Snailbeach mine site about 1900, looking across the 1872 reservoir. In the foreground are the rails that went into Perkins Level. *(KC.Lock)*

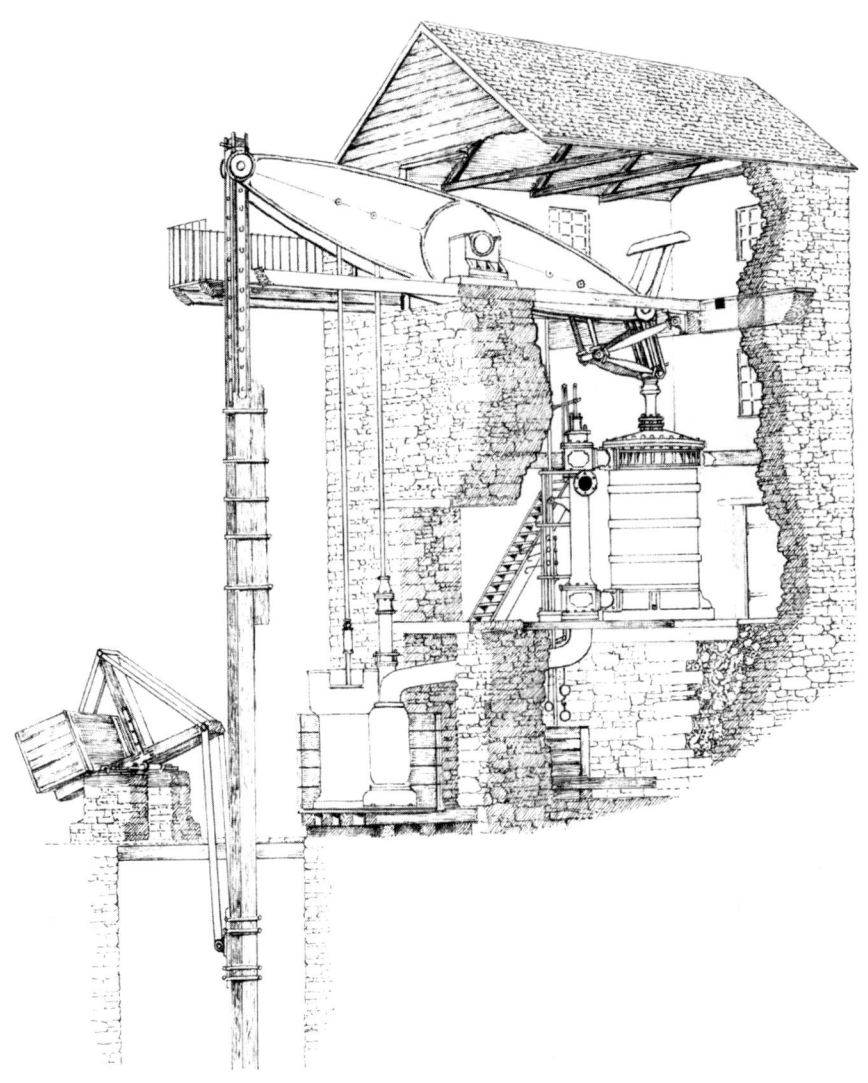

Sectioned view of how the arrangement in Lords Hill engine house might have looked when working. The balance bob (on the left) was designed to ease the load on the engine by taking some of the weight of the pump rods - the box being full of scrap metal and heavy rocks. *(M. Newton)*

Sub-leases of the spoil heaps had been made before 1900, with an engine house being built on the tips to operate the machinery. Then in 1900 the Halvans Company Ltd (Halvans was a Cornish term for waste material) was formed to work the waste tips. When the Snailbeach Lead Mining Company was liquidated in 1912, the Halvans Company then took over the underground lease and mined barite from the upper levels using Black Tom Shaft. The Halvans Company worked the mine throughout the First World War, with the miners receiving a "war bonus" of three shillings per day worked. It carried on mining and processing the tips until about 1928.

After that, Charles Moore & Company (chemists and salt manufacturers of Lymm, Cheshire) bought out the Halvans Company and continued to mine underground. The Gravel Trading Company took over working of the spoil heaps. Charles Moore employed Joe Roberts, trading as the Snailbeach Barytes Company, to mine barite for them from Perkins Level and Paraffin Level (which were above water level). This arrangement continued until 1944 when Joe Roberts bought the lease from the Marquis of Bath. One incident from the 1940s records that men working in the Paraffin Level came out to eat their lunch as it was a sunny day and when they went back in their working area had collapsed. During the Second World War, the miners had permission from the Ministry of Labour and National Service to continue working in the mines instead of being called up to fight in the Forces. Mining was regarded as a protected occupation that supplied vital raw materials. The Snailbeach Barytes Company finally stopped working underground in 1955 and the site of the last blast can be seen in Perkins Level. The miners had been following a fault line but the barite vein had disappeared. The uncleared rocks from the last blast can still be seen at the face, a very poignant sight.

After 1955, the only activity was some reworking of the spoil heaps for spar, to use as pebble dash on buildings. Barite from here was sent to the Windscale nuclear reactor accident to smother fuel cells. Joe Roberts carried on working the tips until the 1970s. Although some ore is said to have been left standing in the mine, the statement "Snailbeach will never be worked again" may well be correct! The old miners were very thorough in their working and rarely left much ore for later generations. Once a mine has been allowed to flood and the machinery removed, the cost of reopening the mine increases dramatically and the prospect usually becomes too expensive. Any large amounts of lead remaining in the area are likely to be below the Ritton Castle area. Unfortunately, miners would probably have to dig at least 1000ft down before they reach the top of the lead deposits, if they could even find them. This is too deep and too expensive so lead mining in Shropshire is unlikely to become a major industry ever again. If mining were to happen again, it is more likely that it would be for zinc. There are large deposits of zinc which were left underground during mining since there was no real market for it at that time.

In the 1950s, various private individuals began to take a serious interest in the history of the mines in South Shropshire - notably John Mason and David Corbyn with his sons. David Adams, as a member of John Mason's group, began a ground survey of all accessible mine sites including Snailbeach in January 1960. With increasing interest in the area he founded the Shropshire Mining Club in September 1961. Later in 1963, a number of records were saved by the Club from the crumbling mine office by George's Shaft. These included a fascinating notebook belonging to the mine engineer dealing with his work in 1858 and his travels to advise several mines in Wales. There were also various account books, sales, letters, wages, cash books, invoices, and shaft rope checking books instigated following the 1895 disaster. These were deposited in the Shropshire Records and Research Centre at Shrewsbury. Efforts were also made to save some of the artefacts in the nearby Blacksmith's Shop but regrettably a number of items, mainly tools, were lost.

Thanks to the efforts of local people, most of the surface buildings were preserved at a time when those in other areas

The 1930s Dressing plant and jig washer of the Gravel Trading Co. The waste tips at Snailbeach were worked by a number of different companies over the years for building materials, including the Snailbeach Co. and the Halvans Company. *(K.C.Lock)*

The Halvans Company Ltd was formed to re-work the Snailbeach waste tips about 1900, finally stopping in 1928. This engine house, on the road up to the mine site, held the steam engine for driving the dressing plant and was demolished in 1985. *(Kelvin Lake-I.A.Recordings)*

By the mid 1980s the Snailbeach mine site was in a sorry state, the headframe over George's Shaft had collapsed and vegetation was taking over. *(Kelvin Lake-I.A.Recordings)*

Weighbridge and office on the 'white' tips. Last used in the 1960s when the site was reworked for 'spar'. *(Peter Eggleston-I.A.Recordings)*

Contractors uncovering the circular buddles on the 'white' tips during site consolidation work in 1994.
(Peter Sheldrake)

were being demolished. Shropshire County Council carried out a series of safety studies between 1985-1990 and acquired most of the land and buildings of the mine in 1990. Building repairs started in 1990 with the Locomotive Shed. The mine buildings were listed as Historic Monuments to prevent further demolition after the Halvans Engine House was demolished "on safety grounds".

Shropshire County Council obtained a Land Reclamation Grant in 1994 to treat the dangerous open shafts and took the opportunity to repair the main buildings as well. The safety work was carried out in two phases; Phase 1 treating the shafts and stopes in the vicinity of the buildings and Phase 2 covering over the white spoil tips with soil and infilling some of the stopes on the hillside. George's Shaft was filled with a mixture of cement and tip material but the brick lining is original. Black Tom Shaft had collapsed above rockhead and had formed a dangerous crownhole. After infilling, the top part of the shaft lining was reconstructed with a grille over the top. Engine Shaft had similarly collapsed and formed a crownhole. Rather than infill it, the shaft lining was reconstructed and left open but grilled at surface and accessed via Day Level. Chapel Shaft was excavated and culvert rings put in place on the rockhead and a bat grille built round the outside. Other shafts have been filled with either no sign remaining or a concrete "Trig Point" structure being left to mark the site. An estimated 8,000 cubic metres of material from the white tips were removed for backfilling all areas and over 2,000 tonnes of grout were injected.

In 1999, a wooden headgear was reconstructed over George's Shaft and was traditionally christened with beer on completion! In 2004, the Shropshire Mines Trust Ltd took over management of the mine on behalf of the council. On 15th November 2003, eight members of the Shropshire Mines Trust Ltd did something that has not been done for nearly 2,000 years. They produced a 190lb pig of lead that was an exact replica of Roman ones dug up in Shropshire. For pictures of this on the internet see :-

http://shropshiremines.org.uk/smt/smtpig/smtpig.htm

Working Conditions

Thousands of people were employed in mines in the 19th Century and up to 500 men worked underground at Snailbeach Mine at that time. Mining was a hard and dangerous life and lead mining was no exception. Generally miners did not live as long as people in other occupations and statistics from the 1860s show that lead miners were twice as likely to die before they reached 65 years old than non-miners. Miners worked in another world, a world without light or warmth from the sun, where water constantly dripped from the roof, and where there was no difference between night or day. The chorus of a popular folk song sums it all up.

Where it's dark as a dungeon and as damp as the dew
Where the dangers are many and the pleasures are few
Where the rain never falls and the sun never shines
For its dark as a dungeon way down in the mine.

At Snailbeach Mine, some of the miners did not live locally. They had to walk several miles to and from the mine every day, through heavy rain, hail or snow, which turned the tracks to mud that clung to boots, making walking more difficult. They were thus often cold and wet before they even started work. When the men reached the mine they changed into their underground clothes in the changing house or "Dry". This had steam pipes from the boilers passing through it so the miners could lay their wet clothes out to dry.

Snailbeach was considered to be healthy for a mine. Samuel Jones, when asked if the miners considered their employment unhealthy said, "no I do not think that they do" but he also added "it is certainly more unhealthy than being on top of the land working". The two main factors in favour of Snailbeach being a healthy mine were that it was considered to be a dry mine, and well ventilated. Much of the water that entered the mine did so on the upper levels, the lower levels were only damp. This was an advantage because it kept down the dust.

The view from the hill below the Lord's Hill engine house looking across the mine dressing floors about 1900. On the right are the chimneys of the 1880s compressor house and the crusher building, on the left is the headframe of George's Shaft, with the Miner's Dry in the foreground - now the Visitor Centre. *(K.C.Lock)*

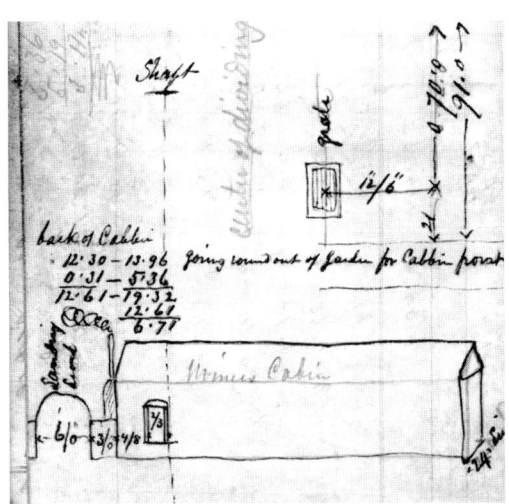

Part of a page from the Mine Surveyors notebook, showing a sketch of the 'Miners Cabin' with the entrance to the "Landing Level" (known as 'Day Level' today). This was probably the earlier 'Miners Dry' dating from changes in the 1850s-60s. *(Emily Griffith Collection)*

Miners working in a large stope. In this example men would climb the ladders to work the ore overhead, dropping the material down wooden chutes to the trucks below. *(M.Newton)*

Many of the levels (tunnels) were large, up to 7 feet high by 6 feet wide, which enabled a good flow of air through the workings. In some mines the miners worked up to their knees in water and in many coal mines the workings were only 2 feet high so the men had to work lying down!

At times of maximum profit, there would be three 8 hour shifts each weekday, changing at around 6am, 2pm, and 10pm. Most mines in the area only worked 6 hour shifts but longer shifts were introduced at Snailbeach due to the depth of the mine and the time taken by the miners to reach their place of work. The 8 hours included the time taken for the miners to go down the ladders and come up again. According to Samuel Jones, a Snailbeach miner, this "occupies us an hour and a half". That was about 30 minutes going down and 60 climbing up. Captain Henwood also admitted that "we call it an 8 hour shift, but the men, on average, do not spend more than 6½ hours in actual work."

On Saturdays, only a third of the miners were at work, between the hours of 6am and 12 noon. The remaining two thirds of the men were thus idle from Friday night to Monday morning. These long weekends were not unusual at the time but were unpopular with the mine owners who still had to keep the mines pumped dry. All attempts to introduce a full day's work on Saturday were as unsuccessful as that tried at Roman Gravels Mine in 1870. The workers from other mines induced the miners there to stop Saturday working by means of threats and intimidation, saying that they were breaking the rules of the country. In 1871, the miners were also taking a day's holiday immediately following the monthly payday. The lunch hour, taken during the shift, was a full hour or more. Both these facts appeared to cause the mine management a great deal of frustration.

Some mines adopted the more traditional method of working called Tributing, whereby very few miners would actually be full-time employees of the mining company. The exceptions were the mine captains, engineer, engine drivers and perhaps a few other specialists such as the men who maintained the shaft. It was even known for particularly skilled captains and engineers to be employed by more than one mine, dividing their time between them. Most of the men formed themselves into small teams and would work a particular stope (working area) of the mine for which the mining company would pay them an agreed rate for a set weight of ore delivered. This was called a Bargain. The men had to compete to sell their skills in a type of auction known as the Lettings. In this, the captain would offer different stopes for a set period and they would be given to the mining team who would charge the cheapest rate for lead ore delivered to surface.

The rate for a particular stope could vary from month to month. If a team found a rich vein which was easily worked, they would obviously make a large profit. This would encourage the mining company to seek a lower rate for that stope at the next letting and this ploy worked because there were always other teams willing to take on rich areas. Conversely, if a stope proved poor during the month then teams would be unwilling to bid for it and the company would have to offer to pay a higher rate before it was taken on. It was always a gamble because, depending on the richness of the vein, a team could either make a big profit or a loss. Surprisingly enough, this system was very popular with the miners who valued their independence and appreciated the chance it gave them to make good profits. It also suited the mining companies because it encouraged the teams to deliver as much ore as possible to surface at the lowest price.

Some jobs did not involve extracting ore and these were treated differently. If a shaft was to be sunk or an access level driven, this was offered to teams at a set rate per fathom of ground extracted. This was called Tutwork. Again, the price for this could vary depending on the softness of the ground being passed through. Another type of payment was day work, where workers were paid a daily wage for a particular job such as unloading kibbles at surface, clearing out collapsed levels or ore dressing at surface. Pieceworking was also used, and set prices for short term jobs. The workers had to wait until the reckoning before collecting their wages and this was a busy time for the mine captain, who had to add up all the ore brought to surface or fathoms of ground extracted. At Snailbeach Mine, wages were

[handwritten ledger extract]

Extract from the Snailbeach Mines Cost book. This entry under 'Tribute Bargins' is for Edward Hewitt & Co. working on the 462 yard level. It shows how much ore they produced and the expenses they incurred, such as candles, powder, gelignite, fuses, etc. *(K. & J. Knill)*

A team of 3 miners drilling shot-holes by hand. One miner holds the drill and turns it after each hammer blow, while the other 2 miners hit the boring tool in turn. *(M.Newton)*

Salop Miners Federation token discovered in the garden of the Snailbeach Count House. *(Lloyd Family)*

A miner's candle stub on the 40 Yard level, still held to the wall in a lump of clay.
(Kelvin Lake - I.A.Recordings)

A typical wooden miners' ladder which can still be found underground at some mines.
(Kelvin Lake - I.A.Recordings)

certainly being paid in the mid-19th Century but it is likely that the bargain system was in use before and after this.

Pumping and winding costs were borne by the company but there were many deductions from a miner's wages before he received his money. At Snailbeach Mine, payments were made every two months on what was called the Reckoning Day. At the end of the intervening months, miners were given "subsist" (an advance on their wages), which was then deducted from the amount due on the Reckoning Day. In the 1860s the miners earned on average 22 shillings per week. Miners had to pay 8d per pound for candles and the same for gunpowder. The men also paid 1 shilling per month for the services of a doctor, which covered their families too, and 9d per month towards a "sick club". This paid 7/- a week to sick or injured miners while they were off work. In later years, the miners also employed a nurse who lived in a wooden house that is on the upper side of the road just before Crowsnest. Miners were fined 2/6d for any breach of the company's regulations, the money going to the sick club. The Reckoning Day was always a general holiday and there was no school on that day.

George's Shaft was used as a ladderway and was described in the 1863 report as a "most capital ladder road, there being plenty of room, plenty of air and easy ladders. I do not think it possible to find a more easy or safer footway". The introduction of a cage to take the miners to and from the 252 yard level made life much less strenuous. The only lighting that the miners had underground was from candles, stuck to their hats with clay. When they were working the candle was often fixed to the rock face, and in the records there are numerous instances of the positions of these candles being used as reference points in the mine. At the end of the 19th Century, the manager at Snailbeach insisted that the wicks be of a certain type. The wick had to be made of three threads of cotton and three threads of linen, folded to give six threads of each. Candles were classed into sizes by the number that weighed one pound. Miners usually used candles at a weight of 16 to a pound.

Underground, the teams had a great deal of discretion in how they mined the ore. This was subject to some restrictions, however, and the mine captain was responsible for ensuring the safety of the mine, having the right to insist that timber supports were installed if necessary. This wasn't particularly for the benefit of the men - he was more concerned that the workings did not collapse and interfere with the profits!

The way that the rock and lead ore was actually removed underground obviously improved over the years as new techniques were found. The mining technique used from Roman times to the 16th Century was firesetting. There is no physical evidence of it being used at Snailbeach, as older workings have been destroyed by later working, but it was the common technique used at that time and we can assume that it was also used here. In this, a fire was lit against the rock last thing at night and the heat would cause the rock to expand. In the morning, cold water was thrown against the rock and it contracted quickly, causing the rock to break up into many cracks. A plug & feathers was then used to break off flakes of rock - two thin iron wedges (feathers) were placed in a crack and a thicker wedge (plug) was hammered between them. In hard rock, progress in driving a passage would be perhaps only 2 inches per day. The ore was then taken out in baskets or sledges.

Gunpowder was introduced into the mine in the 17th Century and this changed mining methods completely. From then on, the miners merely had to hand drill a few shotholes up to 2ft deep in the rock face and blast the rock away with gunpowder. Although this still involved a lot of hard labour, progress in driving a passage could be anything up to 6ft a day, which was much better than the previous 2 inches!

In 1881 the next major breakthrough was the introduction of compressed air drills at Snailbeach. These were originally very crude but they made the drilling of shotholes a lot faster, as well as requiring less effort by the miners. New high explosives like dynamite were also introduced and these shattered the rock a lot more than gunpowder, making it easier to handle. There was a downside, however, in that the new compressed air drills blew rock dust out of the shotholes into the miners' faces. It wasn't until later in the 20th Century that regulations were introduced to reduce the amount of dust produced by passing water through the drill to turn the dust into mud. For many miners, however, the regulations came too late and they were condemned to die at an early age from silicosis and other dust-related diseases. Not for nothing were the early drills called Widowmakers!

Let's listen to some of the people involved during the early 19th Century.

My name is Nathaniel Rowson.

I am 43 and have been a miner here at Snailbeach for 35 years. Where we mine out the ore it leaves huge spaces underground called 'stopes' but we have to leave a few pillars of rock behind to stop the walls collapsing and us becoming the cheese in a rock sandwich! My stope is a typical one and we have four of us working here. We work for ourselves and get paid on what we produce. I'm in charge as I am the experienced miner with my brother Joshua as an assistant to drill the holes. I usually set the gunpowder charges myself but I'm letting my brother learn how to do it as he is thinking about setting up his own team. My son Arthur is the labourer and my other son William pushes the wagons. Outside on the dressing floor there is my wife Emily and my two young daughters Hannah and Jessie. Their job is to break up the ore with hammers and separate out the lead ore. They keep this safe until the month end when the mine agent weighs it to work out how much we will be paid.

Most of the miners here dress in the same way. We wear white flannel shirts without collars, a scarf (which we also use to wipe off the sweat), moleskin trousers and an old jacket. On our heads we wear a cotton skull cap underneath a bowler hat that we make hard with layers of resin. Sometimes we might place a candle on the brim with a lump of clay rather than carrying it. In the jacket pockets we carry food for our meal break and a flask of cold tea.

My name is Joshua Rowson.

I am 41 and my brother Nathaniel is letting me learn how to set off the gunpowder charges. When gunpowder was introduced to Snailbeach Mine weren't the miners pleased to see it! Two men use a hand drill and hammer to drill a 2ft shothole, turning the drill all the time to stop it jamming in the hole. I prefer to use the hammer myself - I get too many bruised knuckles holding the drill, especially if Nathaniel has been out celebrating the night before!

After we have drilled the hole, we clean it out with a scraper and fill it with gunpowder. A lump of clay is used to block up the end of the shothole and a pricker is used to make a hole through the clay for a fuse. Prickers are made of copper or bronze to prevent sparks causing the gunpowder to explode a bit too early. Our fuses are made of hollow straws and in September we go into the fields after the corn is harvested to collect our supply for the following year. We make our fuses in the evening by twisting one end of the straw, filling it with fine gunpowder and twisting the other end. We always check on surface to see how long they burn - so it is our fault if we get it wrong! After lighting the fuse we leg it down the passage and wait for the explosion. After the blast, we have to wait about 15 minutes for the fumes and dust to settle so it is a good chance to have a cup of cold tea and a chat. We then send my nephew Arthur in to clear it up.

My name is Arthur Rowson.

I am 17 and the team labourer. Lumps of galena and barite are very heavy and I shift loads of it about - you have to be strong for this work. If the rock blasted off is too big to be lifted, my dad will drill a little hole and set off some gunpowder in it so it breaks up - what he calls "popping" it. One of my jobs is to put up timber supports if the roof gets a bit unsafe. If we don't the mine agent will get angry and fine us. My main job is to shovel all the ore into a wagon so it can be taken out by my younger brother William. We don't take the waste rock out so I have to stack it wherever I can, either in an old stope or even in the roof supported on wooden bars. I like to watch my dad and uncle work as one day I hope to be a proper miner like them.

My name is William Rowson.

I am 10 and I push the wagons of ore to the shaft, where they are taken up to where my mother is. It is hard work and dad doesn't give me a candle because he says I can't get lost following the rails! I hate it as it is very scary being in the dark and they always kid me that the knockers will get me. We all believe in the knockers in this mine. They make knocking sounds in the distance as we work and we leave bits of our lunch behind for them. All the miners reckon they will lead us to good lead ore or barite if we follow the sound of the knocking. Whistling really annoys the knockers and they will either make the lead ore disappear or make the roof fall on us. I remember when I first started in the mine I was a bit scared and was whistling as I walked along. I suddenly got sent flying by a crack round the ear from my dad. I never did it again! No miner round here will work on New Year's Eve as this is when the ghosts and knockers take over the mine. At 5pm we light candles in all the stopes and leave the mine. My mum says it's just an excuse for the men to go drinking but what do women know!

My name is Emily Rowson.

I am 37 and, although I have to keep the house and cook for all our family, I also have to come and work at the mine for 4 hours a day. This is because our menfolk work underground all day and someone has to prepare the lead ore (what we call dressing it) to sell to the mine owner at the end of the month. It is the same for all of the mining families and we all have an area where the trucks drop off the ore that our own men have mined. I use a flat headed hammer called a bucker to break up the lumps of ore into smaller pieces. I work all year and it is really hard in winter. The only shelter we have is an open *sided frame with a thatched roof. It keeps off the rain but the wind blows through it something cruel. Only men and boys are allowed to work underground and sometimes I wish I was a man as at least it is warmer there! When we are working at the mine we usually wear warm flannel dresses and great coats like those of men, with handkerchiefs round our necks. Also hats or bonnets on our heads to protect ourselves from the weather. Although the work is hard we are always smiling, laughing and singing - it is a good opportunity to gossip to our neighbours as well.*

Our names are Hannah and Jessie Rowson.

We are 6 and 8 and help our mother dress the ore. We take the small pieces she has broken and pick out the whole pieces of galena. The mine owner will only buy pieces that are all lead and he will refuse any that still have rock attached. If there are any pieces with rock still on then we crush it further with buckers. We put this in a sieve, which we shake in a tub of water to get rid of the mud and dust. After picking out any bits of galena we throw the rest away on the tips. Some of the older unmarried girls around here usually go to London in the month of May to work for about three months for the market gardeners. They do weeding and then carry vegetables, strawberries and other fruit to market. They make a great deal of money, which they bring back home for their families. When we are older, and if we don't get married early, we will probably get a job in service as a maid at the home of a richer family. We are lucky to live here though as girls are not allowed to work underground in lead mines. Some of our relatives work at a coal mine and girls there have to pull the tubs of coal underground.

Iron kibbles of crushed and sorted lead ore at the Upper Works in 1968. *(K.C.Lock)*

Smiths outside one of the blacksmith shops at the mine. They would have been responsible for sharpening drill bits and repairing tools and machinery around the mine. Miners would have 'Smith's fees' deducted from their earnings by the Company. *(K.C.Lock)*

George's shaft headframe, with a single sheave wheel. In the years leading up to the mine closure it operated with 2 sheaves wheels and 2 cages - one going down whilst the other came up. *(I.A.Cooper)*

From the mid 1880s machine drilling was introduced at Snailbeach. Initially it was 'dry' drilling, but this produced a lot of dust. A later modification was to pump water down the drill bits from a small bucket, this reduced the amount of rock dust thrown up in to the air. *(M.Newton)*

George's Shaft Disaster

The weather during the first quarter of 1895 was exceptionally severe, with deep snowdrifts making it difficult for miners to walk to work. It was in such conditions that miners gathered for the 6am shift at the top of George's Shaft on 6th March.

The following account, based on the report of the Inspector of Mines Mr Atkinson, gives the reader some idea of the dangers miners had to face from human incompetence at a time when life was cheap.

"... The fatal accident, which cost 7 lives, was caused by the breakage of a steel winding rope at George's Shaft about 6.15am on 6th March 1895. The rope worked in a shaft 252 yards deep and was supplied by a maker of good repute in October 1885. It was described in the invoice as best steel wire rope 160 fathoms x 3½ inches circumference, costing £48 per ton and weighing 16cwt.1qr.10lbs. The rope was put to work on 9th August 1886 and continued in use until it broke, a period of 8 years and 7 months. It was almost solely used for raising and lowering men, the only mineral raised being 30-40 tons of barite during the 6 months preceding the accident. The ordinary work of the rope thus did not exceed 30-40 journeys up and down the shaft per day.

The winding system consisted of two separate cages, each of which had its own rope passing over pulleys on the headgear to the same drum. The ropes were wound on the drum so as to bring one cage to surface at the same time as the other cage was at the shaft bottom. The rope in question wound on a 7ft diameter drum and passed over a pulley on the headgear which was 8ft 8ins in diameter. Both the drum and pulley were too small for a rope of this circumference and they should have been at least 12ft. The weight of a cage and chains was 14cwt and 7 men were allowed to ride at once. The working load of the rope would thus be about 25cwt, exclusive of the rope itself, and this was within the specification.

On the morning of the accident George Williams, the engineman, raised steam and ran the cages 3 times through the shaft as a test. He then raised 2 cage loads of night shift men before lowering the morning shift. It was while the third cage load of 7 men were going down that the rope broke, just after it had passed over the pulley and with the cage half way down the shaft. An examination of the broken ends of the rope clearly showed the cause of breakage to be internal corrosion. It was so severely corroded where the breakage occurred that the inside was practically rotten and not fit to carry the weight of the rope alone. There was also considerable internal corrosion in that part of the rope which fell down the shaft but the part remaining on the drum was still in good condition. The engine, drum, pulleys, cages and conductors were all in good working order and there was nothing to suggest that the accident had been caused by anything other than the internal corrosion of the rope. The latter was examined daily by a fitter named Ed. Edwards and his written reports were always that the rope was "all right". At the inquest, he said that no broken wires were visible and this appeared probable since none were seen on the part of the rope left on the drum or on the companion rope, which had been bought at the same time..."

It is obvious that the maintenance on the ropes was unsatisfactory by present day standards. It was not known when, or how often, they had been re-capped and there was no regular time or person appointed to grease them. Re-capping is a process whereby a short length is cut off the end of the cable where it is attached to the cage and the new end made into a loop for attaching. Edwards said that the rope had not been re-capped for 3 years and the 'rope oil' used as a lubricant appeared to form a stiff crust on the surface without penetrating much. Although the shaft was not very wet, the mine water was said to corrode iron. It was apparently the practice of the engineman, when the cages were not in use, to keep them about half way down the shaft. This meant that the same part of the rope was then always on the pulley and it was at this point that it broke. One of the miners giving evidence said that he and others were afraid of the rope but no complaint had been made.

Conjectural sketch of the scene around George's shaft when the cage accident happened . *(M.Newton)*

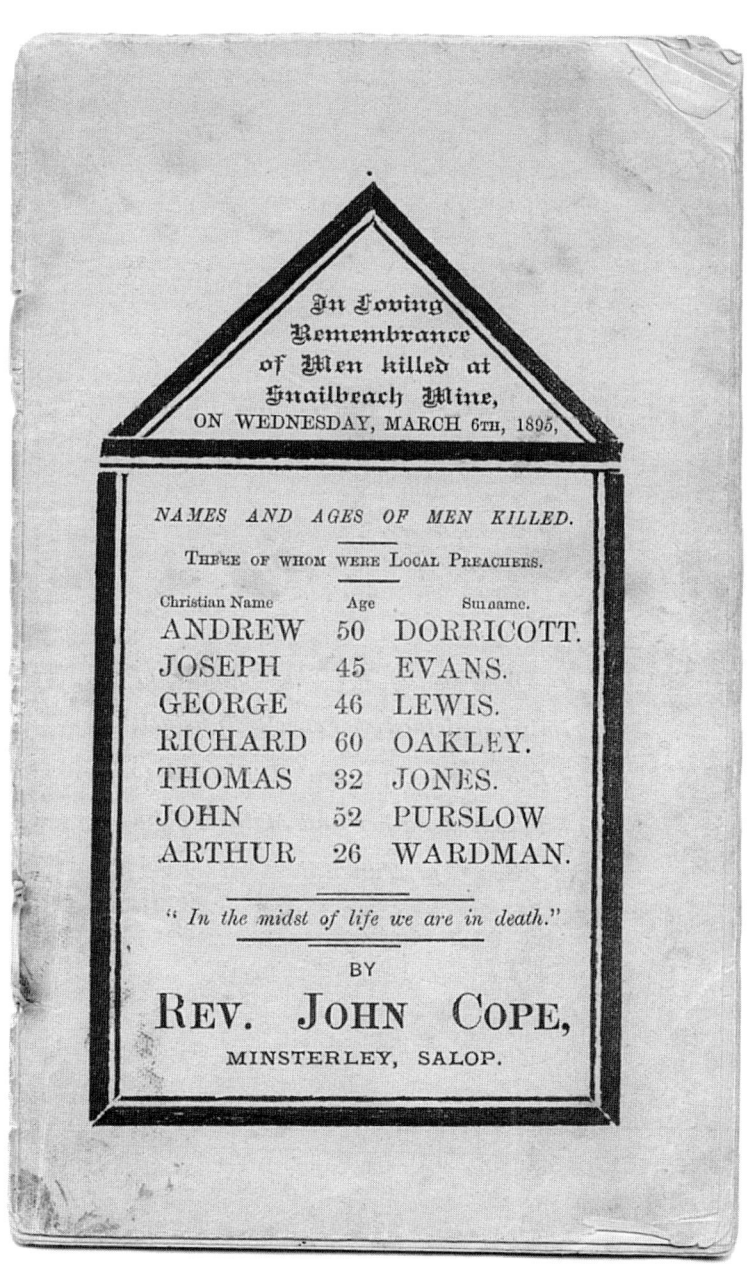

Front cover of the booklet about the Snailbeach Disaster printed by the Rev. Cope. *(Emily Griffiths Collection)*

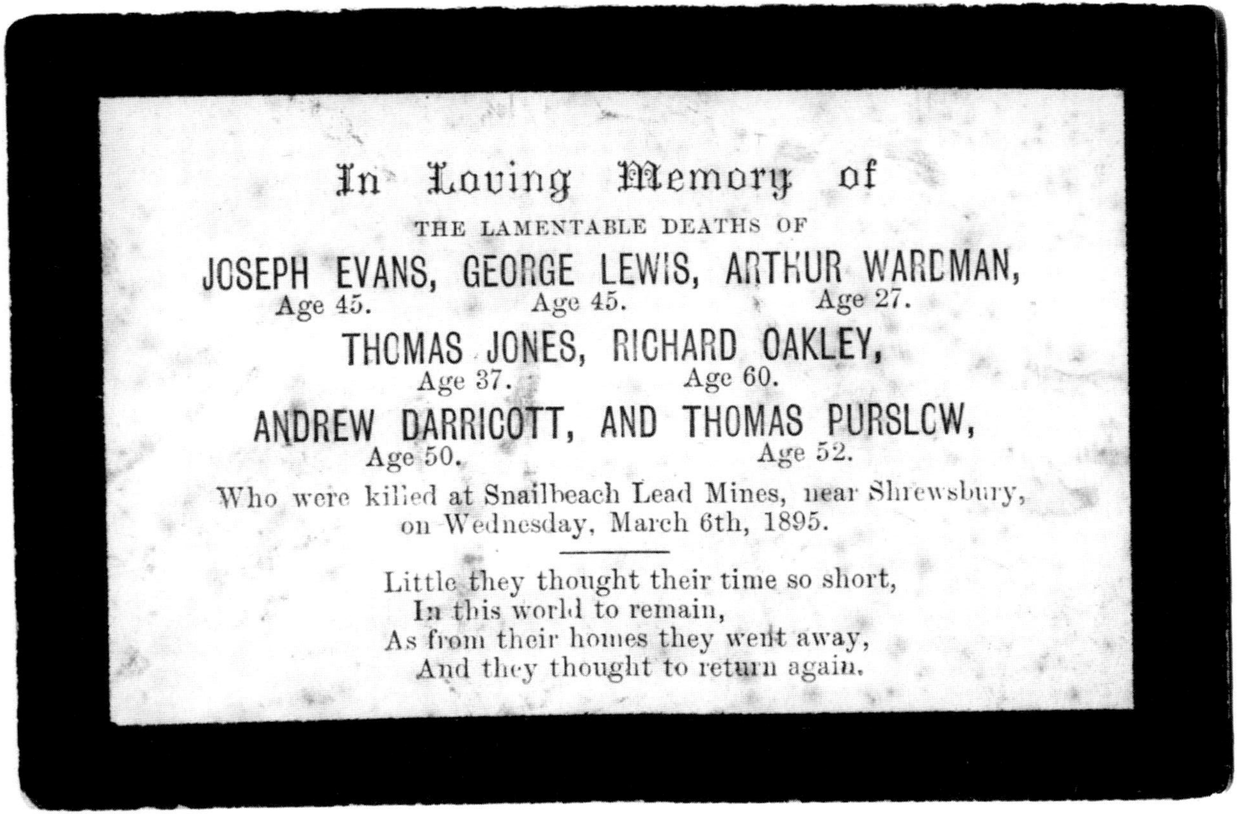

In Loving Memory of

THE LAMENTABLE DEATHS OF

JOSEPH EVANS, GEORGE LEWIS, ARTHUR WARDMAN,
Age 45. Age 45. Age 27.

THOMAS JONES, RICHARD OAKLEY,
Age 37. Age 60.

ANDREW DARRICOTT, AND THOMAS PURSLOW,
Age 50. Age 52.

Who were killed at Snailbeach Lead Mines, near Shrewsbury,
on Wednesday, March 6th, 1895.

Little they thought their time so short,
In this world to remain,
As from their homes they went away,
And they thought to return again.

Memorial card to the 7 miners killed in the 1895 cage accident.
(*Emily Griffiths Collection*)

The verdict was "accidental death caused by the breakage of a defective rope" and the jury thought that the rope had not been properly looked after and had been used too long. Although the Mines Inspector felt that the company and their agents should be censured, there was no breach of the Metalliferous Mines Regulation Act as it stood at the time. More recent legislation stipulates that a winding rope must not be used for more than 3½ years and would probably have required it to be galvanised in these conditions. Re-capping is required at intervals not exceeding 6 months and the pieces cut off must be examined for internal corrosion. This job must be done by a person appointed by the manager and the results entered in a special book. At intervals not exceeding 20 days, the wire must be cleaned, checked for broken wires and examined closely at intervals of not more than 300ft or at other places liable to excessive wear. It is therefore unlikely that this accident could have occurred under present legislation and, if it did, the management could be heavily fined or imprisoned.

The Wellington Journal of 1895 includes a report by W Holyoake, a Snailbeach miner, given at the inquest,

"… I went with seven others down the mine in the second cage. There was no jerk in going down. When we got down we lighted our candles and waited till the next party should come down. In two or three minutes we heard the cage coming down. The noise was like thunder. The cage crashed down with the bodies in it. The cage was smashed up. The rope came down on top of the cage. We signalled up at once and proceeded to take the rope away by drawing it along the level. The rope was knocked about. We had to knock the cage to pieces to get the bodies out. There was no sign of life in any of them. I had every confidence in the rope and it always looked perfectly safe …"

Will Lewis had a remarkable escape as he had already stepped into the cage ready to descend. His father then reminded him that they had forgotten their drills which had been brought up the day before to be sharpened by the blacksmith. Will ran to get them but his place was taken by the unfortunate Arthur Wardman. When Will returned, he was just in time to see the top part of the broken winding rope recoil out of the shaft and nearly behead George Williams the engineman. Members of the day shift waiting at the shaft bottom were treated to the sight of the 7ft 6ins high cage reduced to a mere 18ins by the smash and yet, when the rescue party descended the ladders to recover the mutilated bodies, it is said that a watch worn by one of the dead was still ticking. After adjustments to the winding engine, the bodies were brought to surface in the second cage. Not surprisingly, the miners already underground preferred to climb back up the ladders in Engine Shaft!

The victims were :-

Andrew Dorricott, Snailbeach (50)
Joseph Evans, Perkins Beach (45)
Thomas Jones, Stiperstones (32)
George Lewis, Pennerley (46)
Richard Oakley, Minsterley (60)
John Purslow, Wagbeach (52)
Arthur Wardman, Gorsty Bank (27).

The Rev. Cope visited the bereaved families after the disaster and his "assurances that the exit of the departed was a glorious change" apparently gave much comfort. He subsequently published a booklet about the disaster which concentrated on three of the victims who were lay preachers. He made much of the spiritual guidance they exerted on their fellow miners and their virtuous lives, they were said to quote from hymns at every opportunity. Four of the deceased miners were buried at Hope Church and the funeral procession from Snailbeach was of immense length, even though the journey was long and there was deep snow on the ground. Large numbers of poorly clad miners were reported as taking part in the procession.

Like most mines of that period, Snailbeach had its share of dangers but the general standard of shaft maintenance seems to have left a lot to be desired. The daywork book of 1862 has several references to "boiling composition and tarring wire ropes for winding engine" - not a very effective remedy for preventing corrosion and wear! There was another rope breakage in 1897 but this time the cage was fortunately empty. On this occasion, the 1,200ft rope consisted of two lengths spliced together with couplings. One length, only 2 years old, broke close to the coupling and dropped the cage 120ft.

Rope breakage was not the only danger faced at the mine and examples of two other incidents indicate the type of conditions that would never be allowed today. The reports of the Mines Inspector record an incident in 1897 involving a particularly lucky miner named William Lewis. He slipped off a ladder while climbing up the shaft at the 282 Yard level and fell to the bottom, suffering nothing more serious than a few bruises. An investigation revealed that the ladders were in good working order and concluded that Lewis had been careless.

Less lucky was Thomas Davies who was killed in the engine house in 1896. Davies was not employed at the mine but it appears that it was the practice of local young men to meet in the engine house on Sunday mornings. On the day in question, Davies and others went to the top floor where they amused themselves by riding on the inner end of the beam. He grabbed one of the horns of the beam and was lifted by it but, on the return stroke, fell and was crushed by the beam. The engineman had previously been cautioned by the manager about letting strangers into the engine house but he had made no attempt to stop them. Although the beam was normally protected by a 5ft high wooden fence, this had been removed to clean the bearings and had not been replaced. This is a highly unusual incident since enginemen were traditionally jealous about letting others into their engine houses. They usually kept the brasswork gleaming and the floors swept, barring access to ordinary miners who might dirty the floor or interfere with the machinery. It was in fact regarded an honour to be allowed around an engine house and such visits were normally restricted to management or important visitors.

Apart from the accidents already mentioned, the list below of accidents at the mine between 1875-1930 will give an idea of the dangers faced every day by the lead miner.

1875 1 killed when struck on head by rock rolling down a slope.
1875 2 killed in shaft when they fell from platform
1878 1 killed by premature explosion when ramming a charge
1883 1 killed, 3 injured when drilling machine exploded old charge of dynamite
1883 1 injured when drilling machine fell on him
1883 1 injured when slipped off ladder and fell 23ft
1887 1 injured when spark exploded gunpowder in his canister
1887 1 injured when drilling machine exploded old charge of nitro glycerine
1888 1 injured by falling stone in shaft
1897 1 killed when run over by a wagon on surface
1899 1 killed by moving cage in inclined shaft

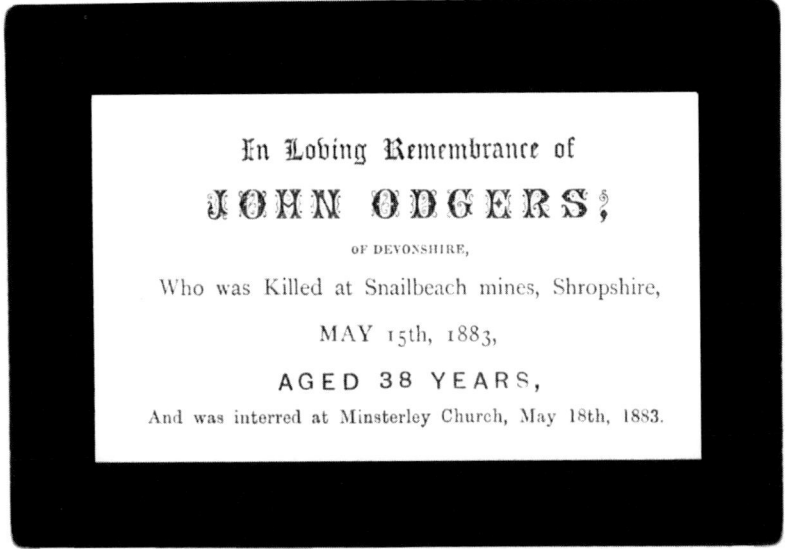

Memorial card to John Odgers a Foreman at Snailbeach who was killed when a rock drill caused the remnants of gelignite in an old hole to explode. Three others were injured, including John Hewitt who was blinded.
(Emily Griffiths Collection)

The Chapel on top of the hill above Snailbeach. One of the victims (Arthur Wardman) of the 1895 accident is buried here. Gravestones of other members of the Snailbeach workforce can be found here, including Vincent Hughes the mine mechanic in the 1850s. *(Kelvin Lake - I.A.Recordings)*

Captain Oldfield, the manager in charge of Snailbeach Mine at the time of the accident. He led the rescue efforts to recover the victims' bodies. *(K.C.Lock)*

Living Conditions

A mine was the centre of a whole community and everyone was affected by its progress. In the good times, everyone enjoyed a share of the wealth but the closure of a mine was a catastrophe that could mean the destruction of the community. Those miners with smallholdings might be able to hang on until the mine was opened up again but many found that they had to move to other parts of the country or even abroad. Adjacent to many of the mines in this area you will find ruins of houses, which were abandoned when the mines closed forever. If you visit the head of Perkinsbeach Dingle or Blakemoorgate, you can see the remains of whole abandoned villages. Some of the miners' buildings, such as cottages, schools, chapels and churches, still exist today and you may be able to recognise them amongst the more modern buildings of villages in the district. Of all the villages in the district, Shelve and Minsterley were the most important from a mining point of view and were local centres for supplies, entertainment, etc. Miners would often travel great distances to find work and a number of the managers at Snailbeach came from Cornwall. After the mine eventually closed, some of the miners went to work in the South Wales coalfield.

It was unusual for local mining companies to provide houses for their workers and, although some miners lived in villages, many more preferred to live in smallholdings scattered over the surrounding hillsides. Landowners encouraged their miners to "squat" on their land and to make small enclosures. In this way, they could collect rent from the miner as well as obtaining his labour. From his cottage, the miner used to walk many miles to the mine, both day and night in all kinds of weather. Each cottage had a number of acres of land and this allowed the families to supplement their income by growing most of their own food. This led an irate mine owner of the 19th Century to remark that, because of the need to cultivate their own land, the miners were not entirely dependent upon their earnings at the mine for subsistence. This was apparently an undesirable trait as it made the miners too independent!

Their houses were small by our standards, with no more than 2 bedrooms upstairs and a living room and pantry downstairs, occasionally with lean-to buildings at the side. The miners built their own houses out of local stone with a thatched roof, with neighbours often lending a hand. It was a tradition that if they could build a stone chimney between sunrise and sunset and have a fire with smoke coming out of it before nightfall then they could stay and finish off the house at that spot. Outbuildings were also thatched but the walls were made with a frame of wood filled with a mixture of gorse, turfs and mud. The smallholding was usually sufficient to provide enough grazing for the milking cow in summer and hay to last the winter, while some miners also kept pigs for bacon or as porkers. These pigs were not fed as scientifically as modern animals and often had to make do with acorns, which had been soaked in a barrel of water. Poultry were common, as were sheep, which were allowed to roam the hillsides. Since the miner's family tended to be large, he was therefore of necessity a keen gardener, using his vegetable garden as an important additional food supply. The children were expected to help out by collecting whinberries and blackberries from as far away as the Long Mynd to supplement the family diet. This was so important that schoolmasters often had to close the local school at those times of the year when wayside fruits were ripe. A miner's main meal might consist of bacon and vegetable stew with homemade bread. To eat meat supplied by the butcher was unusual and this would depend on how much he was earning at the time.

Some families made the journey to Minsterley, Pontesbury or even Shrewsbury, either walking or riding on the horse drawn wagon of the local carrier. In later days the railway became available, although some people regarded it as a waste of good money and still preferred to walk. Local political feeling ran strongly at times and elections were occasionally accompanied by violence between bands of rival villagers. The Hope Valley was a Tory stronghold whilst Snailbeach was staunchly for the

One building still stands almost intact at the abandoned village of Blakemoregate, on the hill above Snailbeach. *(Kelvin Lake-I.A.Recordings)*

Typical miners or 'squatters' cottages can still be seen around the Snailbeach mine site. *(Kelvin Lake-I.A.Recordings)*

A 'squatters' cottage with corrugated iron roof. near Tankerville. Dozens of buildings like this were once dotted around the Stiperstones, most have now been demolished, while a few have been extended and converted to large houses. *(Kelvin Lake-I.A.Recordings)*

Sheep still graze the hills around Snailbeach, just as they would have done in the heyday of the mines. *(Kelvin Lake-I.A.Recordings)*

Liberals. The supporters of each party were in the habit of attempting to prove their superiority by punching the heads of their supposed inferiors!

Compared with some areas, the district was very well served by schools. Although most were small, they were very numerous and each small village had its own. The local free school in Minsterley, founded in 1843, was a typical example of one of the larger ones. It was erected at the joint expense of the Marquis of Bath and several gentlemen of the Snailbeach Company, with accommodation for 100 pupils and average attendance being about 80. The company provided an endowment of £40 per annum towards the running costs and each miner was expected to pay 6d per quarter to the schoolmaster. The schoolmaster's wage would have been £100 per annum (twice the average miner's wage) unless he chose to pay an assistant.

The mining communities were very religious and there was a strong chapel following in the district. It is significant that, of the 7 men killed in the Snailbeach disaster, 3 were lay preachers and the other 4 were steady attendees. Five were Methodists and the remaining two belonged to the Church of England. The Rev. John Cope of Minsterley preached in the district in 1896 and published a small booklet about the accident. This booklet gives a revealing account of the important part religion played in the social life of the community. One of the dead was a leading member of the Band of Hope and spoke strongly against the evils of alcohol "thereby saving the local children from 10,000 sins". Another "preached of Hell as a reality" and a third was a leader of the local Sunday School. The Wellington Journal of the times records that Mr Henry Wiggin of London, known as the "Weeping Preacher", visited Snailbeach and had large audiences for night after night.

Sunday Schools thrived and the big occasion of the year was the 'Treats'. In hard times, these might only consist of marching behind a local brass band, followed by a picnic on top of Corndon Hill. Later trips were made with the children riding in horse drawn wagons and eventually in charabancs to places as far away as Rhyl. The chapels organised Eisteddfodau at holiday times with singing competitions and another popular local activity was football. Thrift was encouraged by means of the Chapel clothing clubs and charity took such forms as paying a child's school pence when the father died.

A Miner's Daughter in the 1940s

It is so cold in this bedroom. When I went to bed I was in the middle, between my older sisters, but now I'm on the edge. I'd better get out of bed and pull the old army blanket and flannelette sheets in my direction. I step out of bed and fall flat on my face, my winceyette nightie is so long I keep tripping over in it. My sister Hilda is two years older than me and taller so every thing that passes down to me is two years too big. Trying to hold up my nightie and pull the blanket is not easy but I do it. Back in bed I am cosy… for a while. Now I need a wee. It's too dark and cold to go out side to the lavvy, so out of bed again, carefully so as not to fall over my nightie. I am on my knees fumbling around looking and feeling under the bed for the chamber pot. "Why can't someone invent a switch on a candle then I could see".

"Our Elsie is that you messing around". Oh no, now I've woken up Hilda. "It's alright I'm using the chamber pot, well I would if I could find it," I reply, "it's by Annie's side of the bed", Hilda says, "so hurry up then get back into bed". You would think that it was a simple task, but no. It's dark and cold and I can't see my hand in front my face and I've got to find the chamber pot or wet myself. You can bet our Annie has left the pot in the middle of the floor. On my hands and knees I carefully fumble for the pot, this damn long nightie doesn't help. Found it at last, I hope it's not too full, because now I'm finished I've got to put it back under the bed or else our Annie will step in it when she gets up. I'm cold and crawling around on floor boards in the dark is scary, as I know there was a spider in here yesterday. More fumbling and I'm back in bed.

Now Annie and Hilda have the entire eiderdown. The eiderdown is heavy as it's stuffed with lots of feathers, but it

Smelthouse cottages, a row of workers houses at the former Snailbeach smelter. *(K.C.Lock)*

Lords Hill & Snailbeach Baptist Chapel with its own burial ground was built about 1873. A united church was formed in 1805 in Minsterley where Baptists and Independents met for worship. However they split in the 1830s, building their own chapels. *(Kelvin Lake - I.A.Recordings)*

Holy Trinity Church, Hope. Several of the victims of the Snailbeach mine disaster were buried here. *(Kelvin Lake - I.A.Recordings)*

Mount Zion Primitive Methodist Chapel, Pennerley, erected in 1869 in what was then a busy mining area. *(Kelvin Lake - I.A.Recordings)*

keeps us really warm. After a bit of tugging and heaving I get my share of it. It feels like I have hardly been asleep for a minute when It's time to get up, I know this because our Annie is bouncing all over the bed. We try to get dressed under the bed covers to keep warm but it's impossible. I quickly (well as quick as you can when there is so much to put on) dress myself, starting with my knitted vest, pants, petticoat, skirt, blouse, cardigan and finally my knitted socks. I feel warmer already. I go over to the window to look out but Jack Frost has been and the window is covered in lovely icy patterns. Using my finger nails, I scratch a picture in the frost. "Elsie, breakfast", that's Mum shouting at me already and the day has only just started. Today is Saturday, so no school.

Saturday breakfast is porridge with a sprinkle of salt on top and a nice cup of tea. Dad has already gone to work at the mine, he went at 6.00am this morning. Mum makes him a bottle of tea wrapped in paper and placed in an old woollen sock to keep it warm for a while. Dad takes his lunch in a tin box and today Mum gave him bread and dripping and the last bit of bacon from the pig we slaughtered a while ago. He has to walk a long way to reach the mine and in summer we run to meet him after work, Friday is the best day to meet him as it's pay day and he gives us a penny. We go straight to the shop in Snailbeach and spend it, some times the ice cream man would be there and we would have ice cream, a real treat.

"Elsie May there's jobs to be done", it's my Mum again. That's the one thing about Saturday, there are jobs to do. Annie and Hilda are so organised, they have already bought up two buckets of water from the well. Mum said its best if I don't get the water so I do the fire grates instead. All because the water just seems to jump out of the bucket when I fetch it and it might take me a bit longer because I have to look at what's about, just in case I miss something. Mum passes me the old sack apron, as if I would forget to put my apron on. With my two years too big passed down shoes on, I dash to the out house to get the bucket for the ashes. The fire has to stay in; it's our cooker and heats the house and water. The ashes at the bottom of the grate have to come out to let some air in. Shovel in hand I start, a few ashes at a time, I'm doing well today cause no one has shouted "Elsie May" for at least five minutes!

The ashes have to go down to the bottom of the garden, to make a path from the lavvy to the house. This bit is bad. I try to slowly tip the ashes but as always the breeze blows them in my face. Spitting out ash and rubbing my eyes I go back to the house. "Elsie May", there she goes again, my Mum. "How many times do I have to tell you, see which way the wind is blowing before you tip the ashes, then stand with your back to the wind and the ash will not go in your face". All well and good but how can you see the wind. Mum spits on her apron and starts to rub ash of my face, ugh why do Mums fuss so much. I finish brushing the hearth, now it's the fenders turn to get it. The fender is Mum's pride and joy, it's brass from my Nana and it goes in front of the fire and makes it look posh.

I use this smelly and I mean really yucky smelly stuff in a tin. I put it on an old rag then wipe it all over the fender. It turns white when it's dry, so when Mum's not looking I make patterns in it with my finger. Then the hard work begins, you have to rub all the white stuff off until the fender shines. This all seems a waste of time to me, putting stuff on then wiping it off. I really would like to fetch the water but I'm not allowed. It was an accident when that bucket of water tipped itself over Annie and anyway water doesn't smell. Oh no talking about smells, I've got to empty the chamber pot. My sisters are feeding the pig and the hens, that's a good job as the boiled up peelings and pig meal smell lovely.

Here I go walking slowly, the last thing I want is to fall and have to clean up all Annie's wee. I have to go all the way down the garden to the lavvy to empty the pot, our lavvy is a posh one and we have two seats, one for us kids and one for grown ups. Which is just as well, because our Annie once sat on the big one and almost fell into the bucket underneath. I'm supposed to check the paper while I'm here; there will not be enough newspaper squares so I will have to go get some. Dad brings a newspaper back from work every now and then, when every one has read it; I rip it into squares and put it in the lavvy. So here I am sitting by the back door on the stool to rip up the newspaper. "Elsie...Elsie May" there goes that ringing in my ears again, "Just what do you think you are doing, the newspaper is blowing all over the garden". And it was, just as Mum said. Oops I must have been day dreaming, "Get it all picked up now and finish what you started". All this wouldn't happen if Mum would let me feed the pig. Anyway we have some proper toilet paper, but that's only for visitors.

Jobs all done at last, we sit at the table for lunch. Today its rabbit stew, and Mum has had the pot on the stove all morning. Dad is good at catching rabbits in the snare and we are good at eating them. Saturday afternoon passes quickly, me and my

The Hewitt Family in the 1890s. John Hewitt (with his eyes bandaged) was injured in a drilling accident that killed John Odgers and injured 2 others. John's son Alfred (at the back on the right) died in 1974 and was the last of the Snailbeach "mine workers". *(K.C.Lock)*

Alfred Hewitt (1878-1974) in the late 1960s, by the collapsed headframe at Black Tom shaft. He drove the pumping engine on Lords Hill until the mine closed in 1911, and then worked in other nearby mines. *(K.C.Lock)*

Mr Randle at the Snailbeach buddles c1915. He appears to be operating a sluice or lever on a jig or buddle. Surface workers were just as much a part of the mine workforce as the miners, often having to work outside in all weathers. Jobs on the dressing floor could be particularly wet and uncomfortable. If the Company didn't provide 'drying' rooms the men would have to walk home, often several miles, in their wet work clothes. *(Emily Griffiths Collection)*

sisters play outside on a rope in the barn. Hilda has a rag doll; we all take turns at playing with it, I'm sure soon it will be my turn to have a toy of my own. Mum shouts to tell us its three o'clock. Great, my sisters and I go down towards the mine to meet Dad. He finishes at 3.00pm and we walk back together. Dad is very dusty and we walk slowly as he's got a bad cough. Working down the mine makes a lot of the men ill. Most of my friends at school don't have a Dad as one way or another the mines have taken them. Last year there was a big accident and men were killed, it was a very sad time for everyone. By the time we get home, Mum has got the hot water in the bath ready for Dad in front of the fire. We girls have a quick bath first; three girls in a tin bath by the fire is great fun. After Dad finishes, we bucket the water out, I'm allowed to take water out, but not bring it in. Anyone would think I might spill it.

After a tea of bread and jam, we sit and talk about what would be planted in the garden as soon the morning frosts are gone. We listen to the radio for a while and then it is bed time again. Me and my sisters run to the lavvy together before dark, you never want to go in the dark as the candle goes out and them two round holes look like eyes staring at you. And no one wants a wee with a boggle eyed monster watching. While we are in bed we can hear Mum downstairs putting out pots and pans to get Sunday dinner ready. Mum and Dad don't work on Sundays, so Mum peels all the spuds and stuff on Saturday. "It's no wonder they don't work as we spend all day walking to and fro from chapel".

No frost this morning but this nightie is still tripping me over. Today we can put on our best clothes, it's chapel. Hilda and Annie look very ladylike but me, huh…in my two years too big skirt and blouse I look like my old gran… I can't wait until I grow into my sisters best clothes, then I'll really look something. Mum looks lovely because she makes all her best clothes. I watch her after tea, she sits by the oil lamp carefully sewing. Mum wears a silver thimble on her finger, it was a gift from my gran and one day I might have a shiny thimble. Well here we go, breakfast over and we all walk over Lordshill to chapel, at least it's a dry day. Dad looks fine and handsome in his Sunday best, I look quite something myself. Hilda said there was quite a resemblance between me and a character in Little Red Riding Hood. Hilda knows I don't read and I don't know that story, I asked Mum about the story and she just told Hilda to shush and said "it's Sunday so think Christian thoughts". But I know I heard Hilda say something about an "old granny".

At chapel every one smiles and welcomes one another. We sing lots of hymns, then listen to a lecture (Mum says it's a sermon but it sure sounds like a lecture to me). I try very hard to listen, I really do! Just at that moment a blackbird hops onto the window sill, just asking to be watched so it's up to me to watch it. He looks wonderful with his yellow beak and black feathers. Before I know it I've sprouted wings and I'm flying. My silly two years too big clothes have become shiny feathers. Swooping over trees balancing on branches, this is great. I feel the wind blowing gently around me, flying is great. Ouch, my ear. "Elsie" Mum says in a loud whisper while holding my ear in a vice-like grip, "You and your silly day dreaming, what on earth you think you're doing, flapping and waving your arms when the minister is preaching". Without thought I quickly say "I wasn't on earth, I was flying". Mum's face goes red and screwed up then she sits quiet, this means trouble.

Chapel finished, children are dashing out to play and I sort of walk quickly and quietly so Mum doesn't see me. Mum and Dad stop to talk after chapel as always. It was my turn with the skipping rope when we hear Dad call us, it's time to walk home. It hardly seems worth going home as me and my sisters will be back at chapel in an hour's time for Sunday School. As we walk up Lordshill towards home Mum is quiet. Dad has to stop a few times to get his breath and Mum looks worried. Maybe she has forgotten about "all that flapping and waving" at chapel. As we arrive home I can smell the stew pot on the stove. Hilda as usual being the goody goody is about to start and lay the table. Then my ears are ringing "I could be a bell, the amount of ringing in my ears" I say to myself. "Today Elsie will do all the table chores and the washing up" mother says sternly. My mouth falls open but nothing comes out. On this occasion I decide to keep quiet, I know this is my punishment for flapping at chapel.

Lunch is over and the washing up done, so we head back to chapel for afternoon Sunday School. Today is a good day for walking, we hear the cuckoo and then we try to imitate it. What a sight we must look running over Lordshill cuckooing at the top of our voices. Back at home again I quietly do my chores, I have to butter the bread and jam and make a pot of tea. The silly tea cosy is having a mad moment and doesn't fit at first. Then I realise that I have to put the spout and handle through the big holes in the tea cosy. Not that easy, Hilda has knitted it and holes were everywhere but mum said it was lovely. After tea is finished we go off again to chapel, I am about to point out to Mum that all this walking is wearing out my shoes but I think better of it.

Thank goodness for eight o'clock and bedtime. There are only so many prayers and songs you can sing and today I'm all prayed and sung out. As usual, the bedtime shuffle takes place, I go in the middle, Mum says so, as I'm the youngest and I might fall out of bed. But no, our Annie will have none of it, she wants the middle tonight. With all the fuss the eiderdown falls off and the corner of it falls in the chamber pot, I just know this means trouble as I forgot to empty it today. It's not my fault it's all that praying and singing I clean forgot. "It's okay Annie" I say quick as a flash so no one will notice the wet corner, "you can have the middle and I'll pull up the eiderdown", more pushing and shoving and we eventually settle down.

Three views of a decorative china mug presented to "Joshua Hughes, Snail Bitch Mine 1853". The Hughes family and their descendants worked at several local mines including Snailbeach. A Vincent Hughes is recorded as being the mine 'mechanic' in the 1850s-60s. *(Joshua 'Eddy' Powell)*

> **WHITEHALL,**
> **PONTESBURY,**
> **SHROPSHIRE.**
>
> TELEPHONES:
> PONTESBURY 25.
> MINSTERLEY 216.
>
> 3.2 1955
>
> **I certify** that, in my opinion, Mr A. Adams
> residing at Snailbeach.
> is unable to follow his/her employment, owing to
> Silicosis
>
> W. B. BALLENDEN, M.B., M.R.C.S.
> J. H. S. PERRETT, M.R.C.S.

Silicosis, a form of pneumoconiosis caused by breathing in fine particles of silica was a major problem for local miners, particularly for the men working the rock drills. This is the doctor's certificate for 'Happy' Adams a miner at Huglith barite mine in the 1930s-40s. *(Never on a Sunday Project)*

After years of neglect the mine is once again 'coming alive', buildings have been conserved, a headframe re-erected over George's Shaft and the area used for local village events and fun days. *(Kelvin Lake - I.A.Recordings)*

Surface Tour

Visitors can follow the route below to see most of the mining remains at Snailbeach Mine. There is public access to most of the buildings but some areas are private ground and these are usually obvious. Please respect the residents' privacy. Three of the buildings (Locomotive Shed, Blacksmith's Shop and Visitors' Centre) are normally kept locked, except on some weekends when they are manned by volunteers. If you want to be sure of seeing inside, you will have to take part in an arranged tour. Park in the Snailbeach Village Hall car park (SJ373022) where there are toilets. The numbers refer to points on the maps on pages 10, 94 and 95.

Cross the road to the sign up to Lordshill, go through the small wooden kissing gate on the left and walk up the hill along the path.

On the left are the remains of the **Halvans Engine House (1)**. The Halvans Company were processing the tips here between 1900-1928 and the engine house was used to operate the machinery. There was a small rectangular chimney, which was actually false, being used for a fireplace on the first floor. In the east wall was an A-frame as part of the brickwork and this was where the drive for the conveyor ran out of the building. The cylinder foundations and a flywheel pit are inside the engine house, these operated a crusher and screens on the west side of the building. The old white tips have now been grassed over but, further up on the left, coarse spoil has been left as an area where geological specimens may be collected.

Carry on up the track and, where it flattens out, go through another wooden kissing gate and cross the road. Turn right along a track next to the fence and turn left in front of a building with big double doors.

The main railway line reached Minsterley in 1861 and the narrow gauge Snailbeach District Railway from there to the

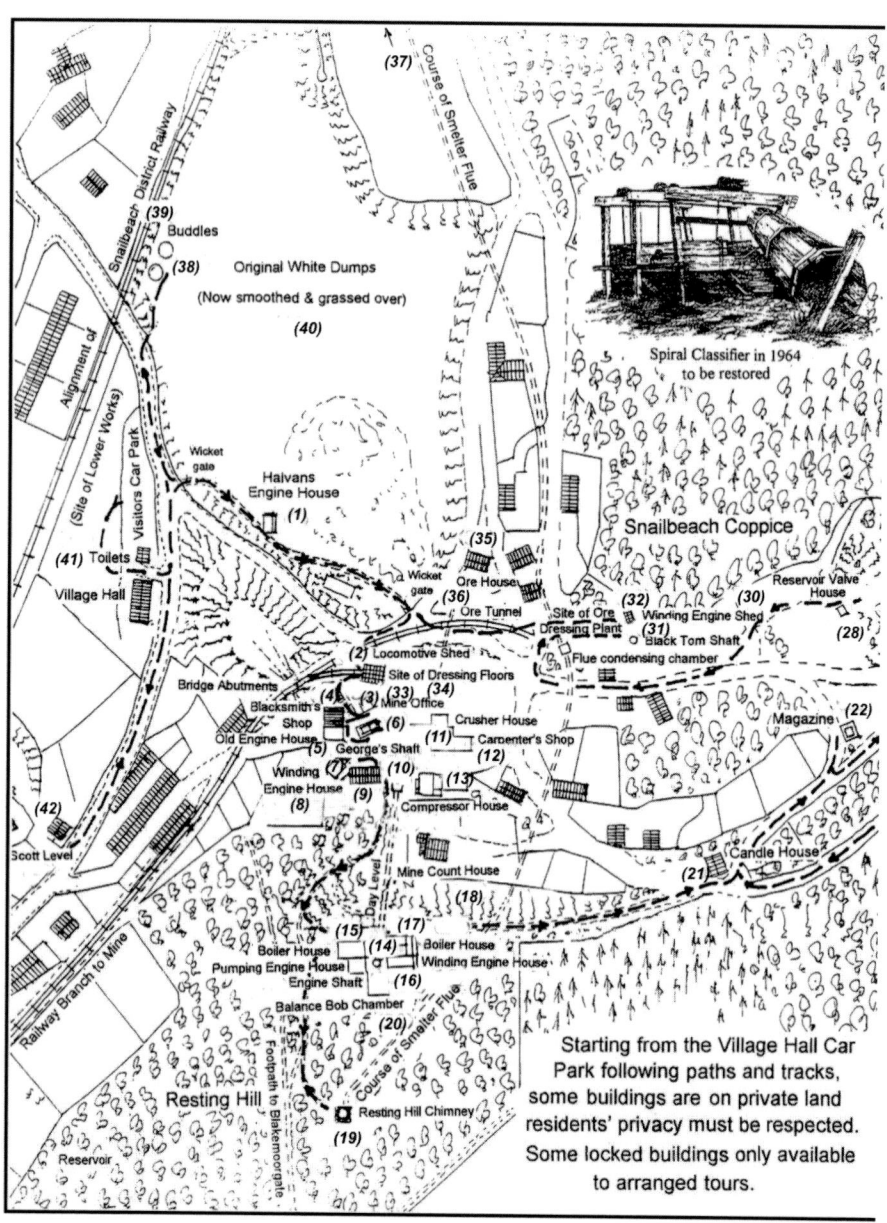

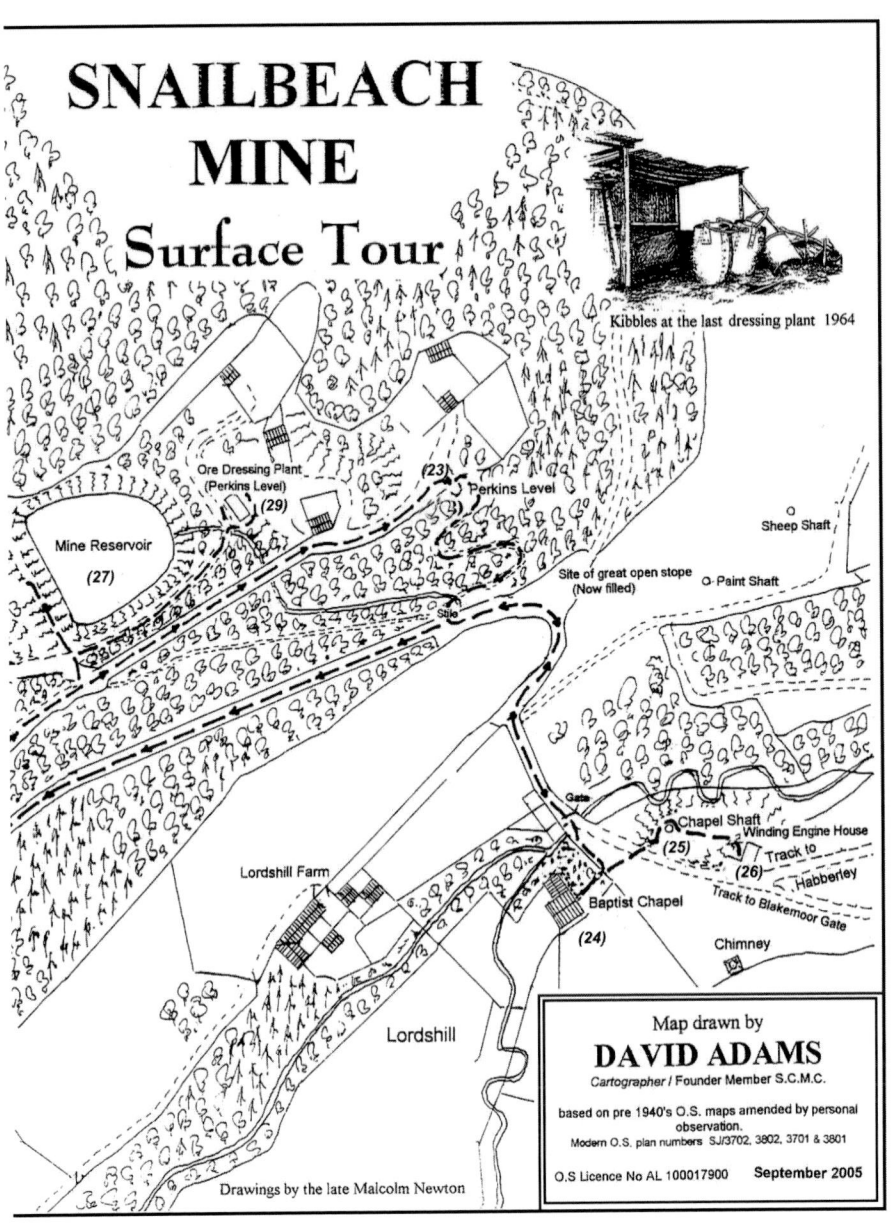

The remains of the Halvans engine house - location 1 on the surface tour. *(Kelvin Lake-I.A.Recordings)*

Geologists fossiking on the un-grassed area of the white tips, near the loco shed. *(Kelvin Lake-I.A.Recordings)*

mine was opened in 1877, to take lead to customers and bring back coal for the smelt works and the boilers. This **Locomotive Shed (2)** was used to house two steam locomotives inside with another two outside. It is normally locked but inside are various displays and equipment. The walls are well constructed of local stone but none of the corners are square, despite the two side walls being parallel. The roof is a double span and was originally covered with diagonal boarding and roofing felt, but was repaired with corrugated iron in later years. During World War Two the two smoke vents were inserted. The two inspection pits in the floor are well drained. In storm conditions large volumes of water pour into these pits but it is not known where these drains discharge. Old photos show a curved corrugated iron canopy with wooden uprights outside the doors, which served as shelter for two additional locomotives, but this has now gone. The original layout of the inside is not known but some features can still be identified. When the building was restored in 1990, great care was taken to preserve existing features, eg sound roof timbers were reused with the existing iron fittings, wooden lintels were replaced with reclaimed timber and the doors reconstructed using the existing fittings.

Go up the steps

On your left is the **Mine Office (3).** On the right is a building with a corrugated iron roof that is the **Blacksmith's Shop (4),** containing a forge and bellows. This is normally locked but the forge has been refurbished and is sometimes lit and demonstrations of metalworking given.

It has been built next to a small stone building, which is the **Old Engine House (5)**. This building is probably the oldest on the site and is believed to have been built in the latter part of the 18th Century to house an early beam engine. Very little is known about the engine but it may have pumped water or wound ore up George's Shaft. The building is rectangular, with the two shorter sides orientated north to south and almost perpendicular to George's Shaft. The building is constructed

The locomotive shed built to hold 2 locos of the Snailbeach and District Railway. *(Kelvin Lake-I.A.Recordings)*

The Blacksmiths Shop. One of at least 2 Smiths shops at the mine, this one still contains a forge, bellows and tools. *(I.A.Cooper)*

Inside the Blacksmiths Shop. *(I.A.Cooper)*

The 1872 winding engine house for Old Shaft (known as George's Shaft after the 1895 accident). *(I.A.Cooper)*

from blocks of local stone with brick edges to the walls and the door and window apertures. The east wall faces the shaft and contains a blocked doorway in its centre. This wall is about 4ft thick, although it appears possible that it has been added to on the inside and does not appear to be bonded through its entire thickness. There is also a small fireplace in the northeast corner that may be a later addition. The south wall, facing the lane is just under 1½ft thick. The north wall is shared with the Blacksmith's Shop and contains a blocked window high up in the centre.

Nearby is the filled **George's Shaft (6)** (750ft), with a wooden headgear that was rebuilt in 1999. It was here that the disaster happened when the cage wire broke. Facing the shaft is the **George's Shaft Winding Engine House (7)**. This had a horizontal steam, double drum winder that was installed in 1872 and scrapped in 1927. The headgear originally had two winding wheels but one was removed at a later date. Behind the engine house is a small **Reservoir (8)** that fed the boilers.

To the left of the engine house is the **Miners' Dry (9)** (now converted into a Visitors' Centre), where miners kept their underground clothes and some stayed during the week. Next to this is a storage building with some rusty wire rope (not the one that broke). The Miners' Dry used to have two storeys with an internal staircase at each end leading to the upper storey. When the recent re-plastering was done, the line of these staircases was left un-plastered and can still be seen. The slate roof had a single louvre, much the same as the louvre to be seen on the roof of the loco shed, and on the southern side of the roof two fanlights. The lower floor had two doors on the northern side in the same position as the doors of today. Note that there were no windows on either floor.

Inside, the floor is made of brick next to the doors and down the centre of the building. Recent refurbishment filled in the unbricked areas but if you look carefully the original layout can still be seen. There were no chimneys therefore there were no fires for cooking or heating. A pipe comes through the west wall from the adjacent boiler house therefore we can assume that this supplied a form of heating for the building in general and for drying clothes. There are no signs of toilets or facilities for cooking and washing so conditions inside the building must have been dire. Lighting was probably supplied by the candles that the men used down the mine. Imagine the men coming off shift after spending some 8 hours or so down the mine. They would have been tired, cold, wet, dirty and hungry and probably had a change of clothes and little else. The sleeping arrangements were probably extremely cramped with the beds close together and little privacy.

Left of this is the grilled adit of **Day Level (10)**, which was driven in 1848 to intersect the Engine Shaft. New rails have been laid in Day Level and underground tours are available on Sundays and Bank Holidays during Summer. Outside this time, trips can be arranged by prior appointment, including being pushed up on a truck with seats! Ore could be unloaded from kibbles in the shaft and pushed in wagons straight out to the **Crusher House (11)**, on the other side of the track. A flywheel pit can be seen that was part of the machinery that worked the crusher. At the far side of the Crusher House was a **Carpenters Shop (12)** and the grilled trench was a saw pit.

The **Compressor House (13)** with its chimney and boiler house is to the left of Day Level. It contained two compressors installed in 1881 and subsequently sold to Gresford Colliery. As with most of the buildings on site, the Compressor House was well constructed with local stone, apart from sandstone lintels. Inside there are massive sandstone blocks which supported two compressors, between which was a large flywheel hence the need to elevate the machinery. There was a timber floor that was level with the top of the sandstone blocks. Steam to drive the engines was generated by two egg-ended horizontal boilers located in the yard next door. Coal for the boilers was brought in on the Snailbeach District Railway and delivered via a siding to a higher level above the boilers. The compressed air was piped underground to drive rock drills and other machinery.

The entrance to Day Level, with the re-erected plaque. *(Kelvin Lake - I.A.Recordings)*

The Crusher House. Materials entered at a high level from the behind the camera, it was then crushed and sent to the dressing floors to the left of the picture. *(Kelvin Lake - I.A.Recordings)*

Front of the 1881 Compressor house. It housed 2 compressors and provided air to operate underground winches and drills. *(Kelvin Lake - I.A.Recordings)*

Go back to Day Level and climb the path just to the left of it. Follow green arrows to the right at T-junction, left at a Y-junction and left at another T-junction. At the top, cross the track and walk to the grilled shaft.

This is **Engine Shaft (14)** (1,205ft) and, although it is still open, it has been grilled for safety. Note that people may be underground here on a tour so please **DO NOT THROW STONES DOWN THE SHAFT**. It was used for both pumping and winding and led to 6 working levels. Pumping in the mine was originally carried out using a 36ft waterwheel in the valley below, operating flat rods to pumps in the shaft. This system was replaced in 1848 by a 60" engine in the **Engine Shaft Pumping House (15)** on the right. Provision for the balance bob at surface is plainly visible and the ground depression between the engine house and shaft marks the site of the condenser cistern. The engine house itself is of massive construction and the lever wall is 6ft thick. Four large gritstone blocks on the floor mark the site of the cylinder, with holes for the holding down bolts going down more than 10ft through the foundations. The pit between the cylinder and lever wall was for the valve gear, worked by plunger rods hung from the beam. The pump was operated from 7am to 5pm each day except Sundays and to drain the mine for 24 hours in summer took 5 hours as opposed to 7 hours in winter. Note that the "dragon's teeth" appearance of the far gable end is not original and was incorrectly done by English Heritage during construction. The original would have been a standard gable with central window. The engine stopped pumping in January 1911 and, after this, the mine flooded to adit level. The engine was sold in 1913.

Beam engines consisted of a massive wooden or iron beam pivoted on the wall of the engine house so that an equal length projected outside as well as inside. The inner end was moved by a steam engine and the outer end was attached to massive wooden beams (or pump rods) that went down the shaft to work pumps at the bottom. The pistons were quite large and operated by steam, the diameter of the piston describing the engine size, eg a 60" engine. Early engines were single acting, ie the piston only pulled the beam down and relied on the weight of the pump rods to pull it back up. The downward vertical movement of the beam at the shaft end was known as the stroke and the effectiveness of the engine could be measured by :-

- Length of stroke - a longer vertical distance meant that more water would pass through the pump each time
- Strokes per minute - the faster the engine worked, the more water could be pumped.

On the opposite side of the shaft are the remains of the **Engine Shaft Winding House (16).** This contained a vertical steam winder with a cast iron beam completely inside the house. It wound ore in the shaft up to **Day Level (10)** using flat ropes. As the level entered the shaft part way down, only simple pulleys (or sheave wheels) were needed on the shaft top. Tubs of ore could be offloaded in the shaft at Day Level and pushed straight out to surface to be crushed. Next to the Engine House was a separate **Boiler House (17)** to the one for the pumping engine. Coal for the boilers was brought up by rail on an **Incline (18)** using a winch sited in a small building next to the track.

The winding engine boiler flue led into the large flue which ran from the smelter up the hill to the **Octagonal Chimney (19)** above. This is the largest chimney in the district and is constructed of red brick resting on a square greystone base.

With your back to the shaft, follow the track going down to the right. Just past the buildings climb some steps on the right and you will find the grilled over **Main Flue (20).** *Return to the track and carry on down until you come to a road junction.*

Straight across is the **Candle House (21)** which is on private land. This is where the tallow candles were produced and stored.

Lordshill pumping engine house. The engine here worked a series of pump rods in the shaft raising water from the lower mine levels to the 112 yard level drainage adit. *(I.A.Cooper)*

The 1863 Magazine building, with its double walls. The explosives were kept in the inner building from where it was dispensed. This design was intended to direct explosions upwards, rather than outwards. *(Kelvin Lake - I.A.Recordings)*

Walk along the track opposite. At a track junction you will see in front of you a square building.

This is the **Magazine (22)**, built in 1863 and consisting of two concentric square walls, allowing one-way traffic of men going to collect explosives. This building is located well away from other mine buildings and houses for the simple reason that it stored explosives and if it did happen to blow up little damage to the surroundings would have occurred. Obviously there was no "incident" as the building still exists. The inner structure, the magazine proper, is 14ft square and originally had a hipped roof, a timber lining to the inner walls and bark on the floor. The miners wore hobnailed boots therefore any exposed ironwork or stone could have produced sparks - hence the inside construction. In the south wall there was a small window with glass approximately 1 inch. thick, a piece of which is now on display in the Locomotive Shed. Presumably it was this thick to withstand an explosion! The outer wall was not roofed and served as a blast wall. Note that the doors in the two walls are not opposite each other – yet another safety feature. It is possible that the inner door was a split stable door so that the men collecting the explosive did not have to enter the inner building. The explosive was originally black powder (gunpowder) but dynamite was used at a later date.

At this point you have a choice. If you wish to follow a slightly longer route with a steep climb then follow the description below. If you wish to miss this part out then skip to **(A)** *below.*

Carry on along the track, passing to the right of the Magazine and past two collapsed levels on the right. Take a right fork next to a house.

On the right is the grilled entrance to **Perkins Level (23)**, driven earlier this century to mine barite when the price of lead dropped. Underground tours can be arranged by prior appointment.

Climb up the steep footpath to the left of the level to the road above (or retrace your steps to the road). Turn left and follow the road up and round to the right and then left and through a gate.

On the right is the **Baptist Chapel (24)** which was greatly used by the miners and contains the grave of one of the men killed in the George's Shaft disaster. On the left is a round walled feature with a bat grille that is the **Chapel Shaft (25)** (1,026ft), sunk by the Snailbeach Mine Co in the 1860s. Beyond this are the remains of the **Chapel Shaft Winding Engine House (26)** which originally had a converted ship's capstan, subsequently replaced by a horizontal steam engine in 1862. The engine house has almost completely collapsed but the underground flue and a small square chimney can still be seen across the road.

*Follow the road back down to the **Candle House (21)**. Turn right along the track as before to the junction by the **Magazine (22)**.*

(A) *At the junction, take the left fork passing to the left of the Magazine. Walk straight across a track junction.*

The large **Reservoir (27)** on the right provided water for the boilers and dressing floors. The small building on the left was the **Valve House (28)** that controlled the flow of water to smaller reservoirs lower down.

Go back to the track junction. Turn left uphill along a track for a short distance, go through a gate and follow a track to the right of the Reservoir. You will come to a wooden and corrugated iron structure

This is the **Upper Works (29)**. It dates from the 1930s and was used to crush and process the barite mined from Perkins Level.

The shaft cap over Chapel Shaft - the grill is to let bats fly in and out of the workings. *(Kelvin Lake - I.A.Recordings)*

The reservoir which once provided water for the mine dressing floors and boilers. *(Kelvin Lake - I.A.Recordings)*

The 1930s Upper works dressing floor, once used to crush barite from Perkins Level. *(I.A.Cooper)*

The small wooden engine house at Black Tom Shaft. *(Kelvin Lake - I.A.Recordings)*

The level itself is much older. Barite from here was sent to the Winscale nuclear reactor accident to smother fuel cells. Underground mining ceased in the 1950s but the tips were re-worked until the 1970s.

*Go back to the Valve House track junction and carry on down the track, passing the grilled entrance to **Paraffin Level (30)** on private land to the right. At the road, turn right and, where it bends left, go along a footpath and right at a T-junction, which will lead you to a wooden shed.*

This is the **Black Tom Shaft Winding Engine Shed (32)** and beyond it is **Black Tom Shaft (31)** (120ft), which was sunk before 1820 and has been infilled with a mock shaft top fitted. It originally had a horse gin but this was replaced in the 1880s by a small steam engine, seated on top of its boiler, which was housed in the small shed. There was a double pulley on the headgear, which has collapsed but placed into storage. Nearby is a circular saw table, the concrete base of an engine and the site of a spiral classifier and set of jiggers, which are being restored.

Go back to the track and follow the rails opposite through the trees to the road.

On the opposite side of the road, the wide flat area was the dressing floor and there are **Jiggers (33)** and a **Grizzly (34)**, devices used to sieve out ore. Below to your right is the **Ore House (35)** and in the courtyard is the grilled entrance to a **Tunnel (36)** that went under the dressing floor. Ore was dropped down a hatch and taken along the tunnel to be stored in the Ore House.

The **Smelter (37)** is situated about 1 mile north-west of the main area and was supplied with ore by a tramway. It is on private land so permission must be sought to visit it. It was

The Ore House, where crushed lead ore was once stored, now used by the local Baptists during the winter. *(Kelvin Lake - I.A.Recordings)*

Remains of the Snailbeach Smelter building. This was connected to the large chimney on top of Lord's Hill by a flue over a mile long. *(Kelvin Lake - I.A.Recordings)*

Interior of one of the Snailbeach smelter flues, ground movement and tree roots are causing the flues to distort. *(Kelvin Lake - I.A.Recordings)*

Inside the water drainage tunnel from the Smelter Condenser chamber. *(Kelvin Lake - I.A.Recordings)*

constructed in 1862 and, rather than build a chimney at the smelter, they decided to build the **Octagonal Chimney (19)** high on Resting Hill some 1,640 yards south. One reason was that fumes emanating from the chimney were extremely noxious and these needed to be kept away from the village and other habitation. There is a record of birds flying through the smoke from the smelter chimney at Pontesford falling out of the sky. Also, having the chimney here obviously increased the draught and efficiency at the smelter.

The flue from the Smelter to the Octagonal Chimney was made by digging out a deep trench, building a 6ft high brick arch in it and covering this with soil. This must have been an expensive and onerous task as this all had to be done by hand. A condensing chamber was constructed close to the smelter so that any vaporised lead and other products could be washed out using water and run into settling ponds. Because the flue is concealed underground, its course cannot easily be followed but it runs round the eastern side of the White Tip before climbing the hill to pass to the left of the Engine Shaft complex. Over time, lengths of the flue have been removed or deliberately collapsed, especially through the fields to the north of the White Tip and the section between the chimney and the track to the Engine House. Much of the remainder is thought to be open but not accessible.

Walk back down the hill and turn right along the road to the bridge. Go through the gate on the right.

On the left are some circular **Buddles (38)**, which were used to separate small particles of lead ore from waste material. Beyond the buddles, you can see the cutting for the **Snailbeach District Railway (39)** where it passes under the road bridge.

In the other direction is a large area of grass now used for grazing but this was once the **White Tips (40)**, now covered over with 2ft of soil. The tips used to be a well-known local landmark and covered an area of about 11 acres, easily seen

The old buddles uncovered at the bottom of the 'white tips' in the 1990s, now preserved. *(Kelvin Lake - I.A.Recordings)*

The entrance to Scott Level. *(Kelvin Lake - I.A.Recordings)*

from afar. It was made up of waste material derived from the processing of the ore from the mine. During the 1950s and up to the 1980s, the tip was reworked intermittently for the recovery of gravel for use in pebble dashing, driveway surfacing and other situations where gravel was needed. During the land reclamation studies done by the County Council in the late 1980s, it was found that the tip was the source of serious contamination with tip material being blown and washed around the village and surrounding countryside. Vegetation did not grow on the tip because of the very high zinc content which is poisonous to plants. Incidentally lead is not toxic to plants. There was, however, a history of cattle being poisoned with lead ingested from dust on the vegetation. It was decided to leave the tip where it was but to reshape and cover it.

Head back towards the car park.

The flat area on the right now used for parking used to be the **Lower Works (41)**, where smelted lead and later ore was stored prior to being loaded on railway trucks.

Follow the road for about 150 yards past the Village Hall until you see a footpath on the right, leading down to the left of house No.34 next to the road.

The gated portal of **Scott Level (42)** is to be found on the right hand side. It is not known when this level was driven but it may date from the 18th Century as the first part is hand picked. It does not, however, link up with any of the workings of Snailbeach Mine so may have been a trial.

This is the end of the main site but you can visit further features if you wish as below.

Wagbeach Level (43) *[SJ364025]* was the drainage level of the mine and lies in the Hope Valley. Here are the remains of the iron sluice device for a 36ft waterwheel that drove the pumps to drain the mine. These are on private land but a footpath goes close to it. The level is 1,200 yards long and is the only known level to actually drain the mine, although another one from Minsterley was started but never finished. This level was probably driven in the 1780s and intercepts the mine at the 112 Yard level. Later it was driven further to connect with New Engine Shaft. As the mine started to be worked below the drainage level, additional means of de-watering were needed. A waterwheel was constructed at the adit entrance and this motion was converted into a horizontal direction by using a rocker beam (or L-bob), with flat rods running all the way up the level to a sump. Here, a further rocker beam converted the motion to a vertical direction and this operated pumps, which raised water to the drainage level. Eventually, in 1848 a 60" Cornish pumping engine replaced the waterwheel. Traces of the surface leat that carried water to the wheel can be found nearby. It was found to be discharging 5,000 gallons of water per hour when pumping ceased at the mine in 1911 and the mine had flooded to adit level.

Maddox Coppice Mine (44) [SJ382031] is in the Forestry Commission woodland but lies next to a public path. It was an extensive trial level for the mine and has two levels above and below the track.

Nag's Head Colliery (45) [SJ408062] is on private land and lies hidden by hedges behind the Nag's Head Inn. The engine house is still standing but in a ruinous state. The shaft is blocked and no other obvious features can be seen.

Pontesford Smelter (46) [SJ409061] still exists but the buildings are now used as Wynnstay Stores. On the opposite side of the road, the long farm building was once another smelter used by Bog Mine. A short distance along the road there is a stile in the coppice on the right, leading into a field.

Follow the line of the coppice back for a few yards and you can see the base of the smelter chimney.

Cross Guns Inn (47) [SJ369015] is now a private house, on the left before the 1st bend at Crowsnest travelling from Snailbeach. It was once a popular meeting place for local miners.

Central Stores (48) [SJ368015] is now a private house, on the right after the 2nd bend at Crowsnest travelling from Snailbeach. It opened in 1881 and sold tools and other goods to local miners, being run by Enoch Parry who was the ex-agent of New Central Mine. The house next door used to be the mine engine house and the square stump chimney can easily be seen. The shop finally closed in 1953.

Blakemoorgate (49) [SJ378012] is the site of a small community where miners once lived. One of the cottages is still in good condition while others are now piles of stones.

Snailbeach District Railway *[SJ370015 to SJ393063]* still exists as a rail bed which can be seen at several places between Snailbeach and Pontesbury but most of it is on private land.

I A Recordings

I A Recordings is a partnership of 3 enthusiasts who make video records of working industry as well as the remains of past industries. They produce these in a number of excellent DVDs, a list of which can be found at the website below.

They have made several DVDs of Snailbeach and other Shropshire mines and the DVD in the mine visitor centre was produced by them.

http://www.iarecordings.org/

Underground Tour

It must be noted that there is no unaccompanied public access to any of the underground workings and the entrances are either filled, capped or gated. It is dangerous to explore underground without the correct equipment and an experienced guide. Considerable experience of caving vertical access techniques are required to explore the more interesting parts of Snailbeach Mine but the complexities and remains make this all worthwhile. The following description is not intended to encourage you to go underground but, if you have a desire to do this, you can either join in on a guided tour of the easier levels or join the Shropshire Caving & Mining Club if you wish to be trained in the techniques necessary to go deeper.

Snailbeach Mine was worked down to a lowest recorded level of 1,650ft below the top of George's Shaft. However, all of the workings below 112 Yard Level are now flooded and we can only wonder at the extent of workings that will never be accessed again.

The mines were working a long vein, running roughly from the west to east and near vertical but hading (angled) such that the deeper workings are south of the shallower workings. The western end of the workings are running towards the Hope Valley while the eastern workings run into the hillside towards the Long Mynd.

As previously noted, depths in Snailbeach mine were traditionally measured from the top of George's Shaft but the underground workings that are now easily accessible to the public were dug later and are actually higher than the top of George's Shaft.

DAY LEVEL (SJ37450213)

Day Level is relatively short and was driven in 1848 to give access to Engine Shaft to allow ore-filled trucks to be taken straight to the Crusher House. Part way along Day Level, the

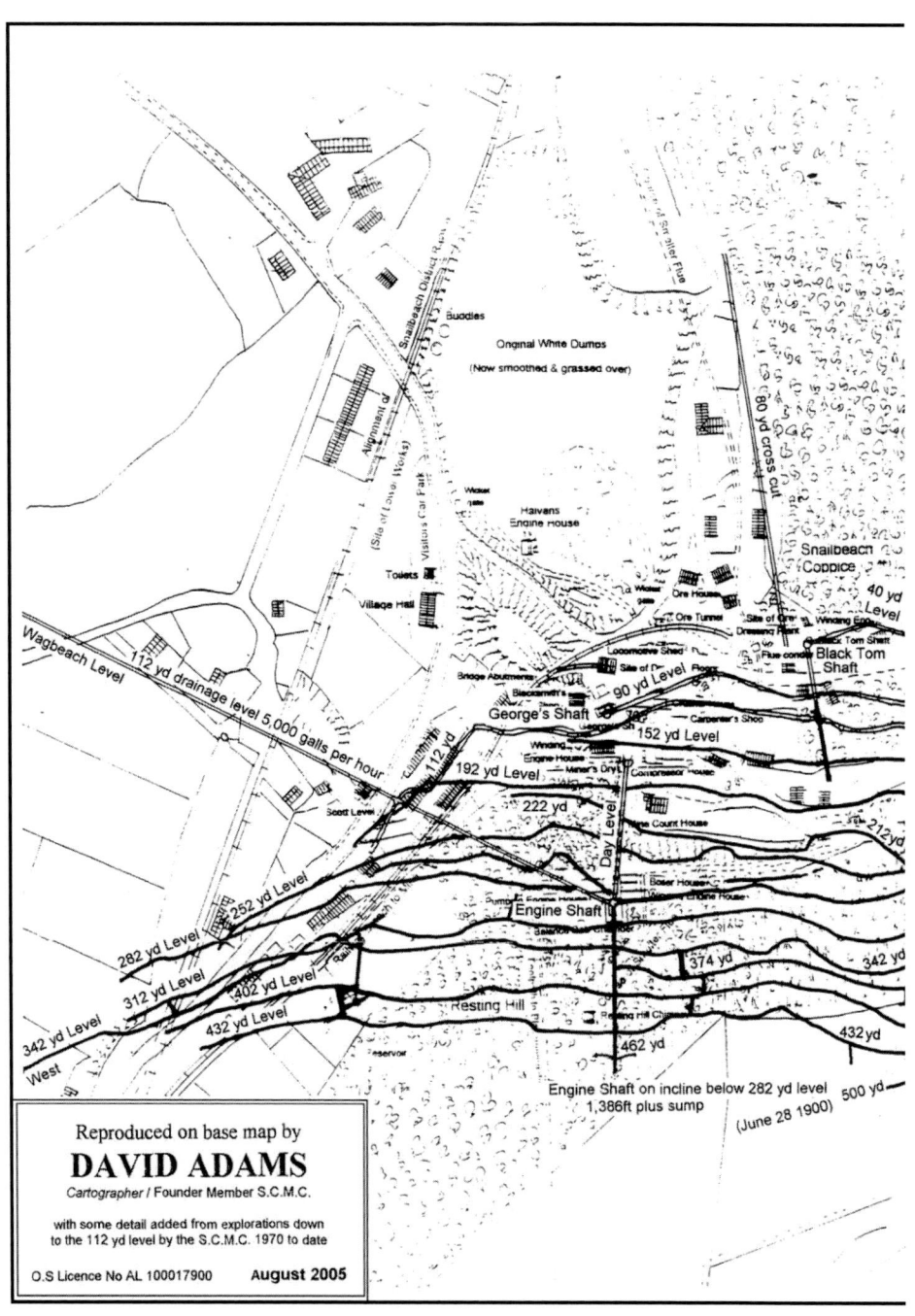

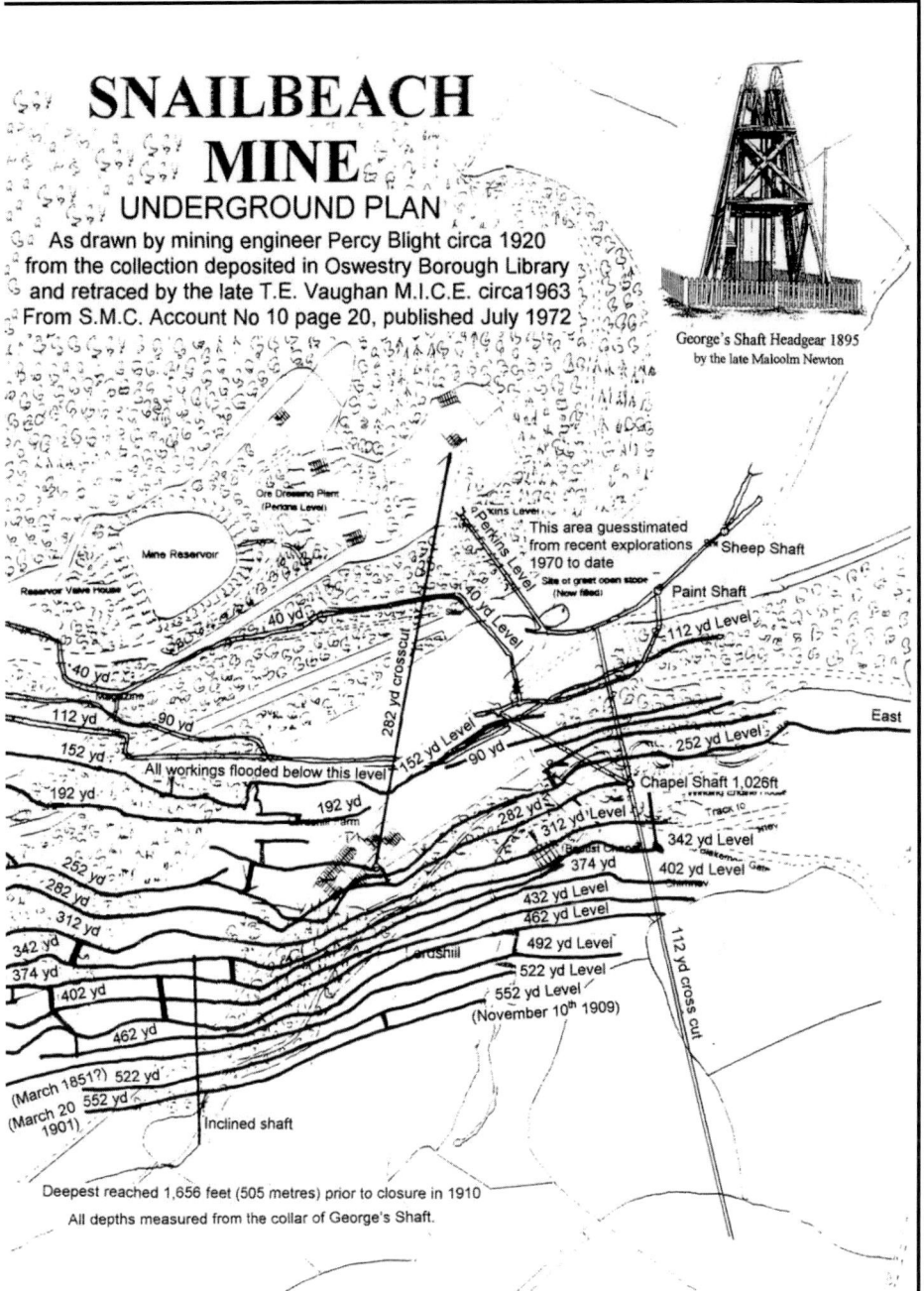

roof is lower for a distance. This is a part of the level where the stone lining had given way but it was re-dug and fully braced during the 1990s reclamation work.

Members of Shropshire Mines Trust Ltd have laid rails again and visitors can now either walk in or be pushed in on a truck. The level is perfectly straight and the only features of mining interest are at the intersection of the level with Engine Shaft. At this point, the level opens into a reasonably sized chamber with daylight streaming down the shaft. The continuation of the shaft to depth is now protected by a grill – so visitors are quite safe. In the wall near the shaft, there are many short drill holes, evidence that this area was used to test drilling machines when compressed air arrived.

Engine Shaft was descended in the 1990s at the time of the reclamation work being carried out. The explorers at this time landed on a cone of rubble but could drop down this to access parts of the 112 Yard Level but this was flooded to the roof after a short distance.

PERKINS LEVEL (SJ37870224)

Perkins Level is the last site of active mining, being worked until 1955. Today visitors are taken into Perkins Level to try and give them some feel for what a working metalliferous mine was really like. These later workings are believed to have been mainly for barite but there is clear evidence of some galena (lead-ore) being recovered as well.

Upper Section

Walking into the mine, first of all note the (now capped) ventilation shaft a few yards in and the original rails – some still in place but most cast to the side of the level.

After a hundred yards or so there is a branch to the right, through a modern corrugated roof section. Following this branch gives access to a large stope (worked out area) – a powerful light is useful to show the remains of a broad barite vein, with pillars and stemples left in place. The passageway continues beyond the Barite Stope to the entrances of other

Rails in Day Level leading to Engine Shaft, now used to convey mine visitors. *(Kelvin Lake - I.A.Recordings)*

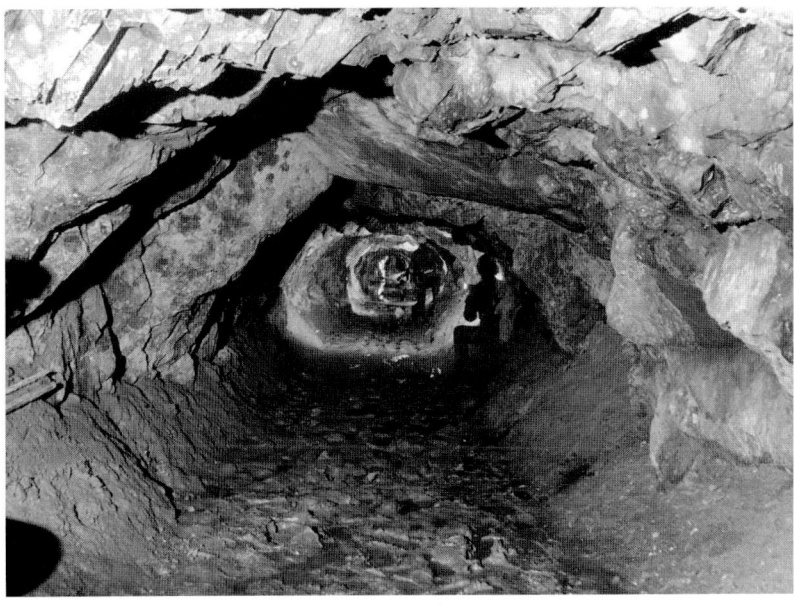
View along Perkins Level, looking into the mine ('in-bye'). Visitors are taken in here on special occasions. *(Kelvin Lake - I.A.Recordings)*

A miner's chain ladder discovered on the 40 Yard level at Snailbeach, now in the upper Barite Stope for visitors to see. *(Kelvin Lake - I.A.Recordings)*

A barite pillar left by the miners to support the 'hanging' wall (on the right) in the upper Barite Stope. *(Kelvin Lake - I.A.Recordings)*

The upper Barite Stope which is connected to Perkins Level. *(Kelvin Lake - I.A.Recordings)*

stopes that were filled during the reclamation work. Continuing further along this passage there is little evidence of successful mining and the remainder of this passage appears to be a 'trial', looking for further ore – various short branches similarly fail to locate ore and eventually the passage ends at the last site of trial blasting.

Returning to the junction of the branch to the Barite Stope, why is there a corrugated roof at this point? Up until the 1990s reclamation work, the turn to the Barite Stope was actually a rough hewn gap in the passage wall leading to a narrow wooden bridge over mine workings disappearing to depth. During the 1970s, this point was used by members of Shropshire Caving & Mining Club to access the 40 Yard Level (see later). Beyond the wooden bridge, there wasn't an even floor like today; instead there was something of a three-dimensional maze that extended below the current floor.

Back to the junction and continuing along the main passageway, another couple of sections of corrugated roof are passed through. These were re-opened as part of the 1990s reclamation work. In the 1970-80s explorers from Shropshire Caving & Mining Club separately accessed the Barite Stope and outer workings via the existing adit entrance but workings further into the mine had to be accessed via open shafts on the hillside.

The collapses were due to the closeness of the passage wall to open workings that used to emerge at the surface adjacent to the road up to the Baptist Chapel and various farms. It was further collapses of these workings and the road that contributed to the decision to carry out the 1990s reclamation works and to the stopes beyond the Barite Stope being filled.

Further along the main passage, yet another longer section of corrugated roof is reached. At this location, prior to the reclamation work, there were flooded workings, complete with ladders and skip-rails disappearing into the depths of water. Also at this location there were open stopes above with visible ladders reaching into workings than were not far below the surface.

A flat-bed mine truck, like the one in the old Blacksmiths photograph, probably used to transport drill rods, etc. into the mine. *(Kelvin Lake - I.A.Recordings)*

To reach the mine workings below Perkins Level explorers have to resort more technical means. *(Kelvin Lake - I.A.Recordings)*

Continuing along the main passageway leads to an area where there is now a metal bridge. This is over the main route down to the lower workings (which are described later). Again, prior to the reclamation work, this section could only be crossed by walking astride the original rail tracks suspended precariously above the depths.

Beyond the metal bridge, the passageway leads to a very large chamber. In places, this chamber is probably 70ft high and 120ft long x 50ft across. Unfortunately, even a small stone falling that distance could cause serious injury and it is not currently safe to allow access to the public to view this impressive area. This large chamber is an important winter bat roost and this is one reason why the area was not in-filled as part of the reclamation works. There are two shafts on the hillside that give access to this large chamber. These shafts now have distinctive bat grills over them and these give some idea on the surface of the location of this chamber.

Some idea of what these 'inner workings' were like prior to the reclamation works can be seen from a video produced by IA Recordings (in collaboration with SCMC).

Lower Section

To the experienced mine explorer, the real interest in Snailbeach Mine is to be found in the levels below Perkins Level. To reach these areas it is necessary to become competent in the vertical access techniques used by mine explorers and cavers. Today this access is normally via Perkins Level but it is also possible to use a winch down Chapel Shaft.

40 Yard Level

It is the 40 Yard Level that is most visited by the mine explorers. Although this is 40 yards (120 feet) below the top of George's Shaft, it is more like 200ft below Perkins Level or 350ft below the top of Chapel Shaft. Mine explorers now usually follow a complex route, involving a significant amount of rope-work, to descend from the metal bridge in Perkins Level.

Descent from Perkins Level brings the mine explorer to one end of the 40 Yard Level. Immediately there is a substantial drop into the depths of the mine where the main working of the galena vein has left a vast open space. Explorers have descended from near here directly down to the 112 Yard Level but vertigo overcomes many and a different (less direct) route is now usually preferred.

This part of the 40 Yard Level is mainly running parallel to the open void but actually separately dug, with just occasional access to the open workings. Travelling along the 40 Yard Level, there is a branch leading to the base of what are believed to be higher workings now collapsed, or back-filled, and not accessible. Following the main level, there is first an area where it again opens into the main stope and the explorer needs to clip on to a safety rope while passing. Shortly after this a major branch away from the workings is reached. This is the cross-cut to Chapel Shaft.

The branch to Chapel Shaft is quite large and often has a strong breeze blowing through. The branch is around a hundred yards long and simply gives access to the shaft. Visiting today helps demonstrate how well the ventilation works. It is interesting to note that there are rails both in the main 40 Yard Level and the branch to Chapel Shaft but they do not actually join – presumably on the rare occasions that anything was trammed in from Chapel Shaft, it would be necessary to man-handle the trucks onto the rails on the main level.

In the late 1990s, Shropshire Caving & Mining Club constructed a plank platform jutting out into Chapel Shaft to assist anybody descending in a cage but this is still suspended over a 100ft+ drop and is definitely scary. Around the mouth of the level into the shaft there are various original mining artefacts including wire cable, diverse metal objects and the remains of a largely wooden wheel barrow.

Back to the main 40 Yard Level, further travel encounters a variety of mining artefacts including a riddle, a device for measuring lengths required for stemples etc. and a collection of shovels, forks, drills and an enamelled powder flask.

On the 40 Yard Level a number of artefacts survive, including these 2 end-tipping mine trucks, partially full of ore near to an underground workshop. *(I.A.Cooper)*

Members of the Shropshire Caving & Mining Club taking a lunch break in the underground workshop, where generations of miners have probably done the same thing before them. *(Kelvin Lake - I.A.Recordings)*

An interesting blue enamelled flask, still holding liquid on the 40 Yard Level. *(Kelvin Lake - I.A.Recordings)*

A collection of miners' tools on the 40 Yard Level, including tamping rods for shotholes, shovels and a 'frank' (a large fork) used to sort crushed ore. *(Kelvin Lake - I.A.Recordings)*

Further along the 40 Yard Level, there is an inset that has probably been used as both an eating area and a small workshop. There is a considerable collection of tools of all types, an aluminium powder container and significant amounts of explosive fuse. This location is also a junction in the level and there are the remains of two trucks. One truck has degraded significantly over recent years but the other is filled and partly buried with spoil and this has helped keep it intact.

One branch at the workshop eventually leads to a blind shaft and is blind beyond the shaft. There are minor workings along this branch but it looks as if it has largely been exploratory workings. The other branch shortly crosses the main stope (current mine explorers having to balance on loose rails while being clipped into a safety line) and then travels a considerable distance towards Black Tom Shaft. It is believed that this level was dug in the early 20th Century to allow the earlier 40 Yard Level workings to be accessed from Black Tom Shaft. Along this connection there are various trial levels but no significant ore-bodies appear to have been located. For later 20th Century explorations, the connection has been blocked before Black Tom Shaft is reached.

Before reaching the blockage, a shaft to surface is obvious and this continues as a dog-leg down to the 90 Yard Level. The shaft to surface is now back-filled but its location is marked on surface by a 'trig point' near the Reservoir. The dog-leg down to the 90 Yard Level is still open. There is a vertical shaft of approximately 100ft with plenty of wooden ladder debris at the base. At the base of this shaft is a short level section of 15ft and then an angled connection of around 50ft down to the 90 Yard Level.

90 Yard Level

The descent from the 40 Yard Level accesses the 90 Yard Level on a short cross-cut which brings the explorer to the main 90 Yard Level passage stretching off in both directions. Turning left, there follows a further 66 foot descent to the 112 Yard Level. Both ends of the 90 Yard Level include areas for potential further exploration.

Members of the Shropshire Caving & Mining Club examining some of the artefacts on the 40 Yard Level. *(Kelvin Lake - I.A.Recordings)*

Members of the SCMC on the 40 Yard Level, using old rails to cross the main stope. *(Kelvin Lake - I.A.Recordings)*

Fragment of an old 'T'-shaped rail found on the 90 Yard Level. *(Kelvin Lake - I.A.Recordings)*

SCMC members surveying on the 90 Yard Level.
(Kelvin Lake - I.A.Recordings)

SCMC members exploring the 90 Yard Level. Note the interesting shape to the level. *(Kelvin Lake - I.A.Recordings)*

Due to a collapse near Engine Shaft, which has blocked the route to the drainage adit, the 112 Yard Level is a little wet. *(Kelvin Lake - I.A.Recordings)*

112 Yard Level

Descent from the 90 Yard Level to the 112 Yard Level again ends in a short cross-cut from a main passage. As previously noted, the 112 Yard Level drains via an adit at Wagbeach. There will inevitably be various collapses going towards the Wagbeach adit (around ¾ mile away) and this part of the 112 Yard Level has always been partly flooded. The author of this section once abseiled down to find the water deeper than he is tall and there was a difficult switch of equipment from descent to ascent while floating!

Exploration out-bye (towards Wagbeach Adit) in deep water has accessed an area with open stoping above but ending at a point where the passage is blocked by collapsed large timbers. Digging of this would not be that difficult if access did not involve considerable time and effort to reach this point.

Exploration in-bye (away from Wagbeach Adit) is in progressively shallower water and eventually leads to a branch. The floor immediately disappears in the left-hand branch (and this will be the lower flooded stopes) – the other side of these flooded stopes are the areas accessed by direct descent from the 40 Yard Level, near the branch to Chapel Shaft, and all passages lead to blind headings.

The right-hand branch gives access to a chamber that is intersected by Chapel Shaft and then continues for a very considerable distance (approximately in a south-easterly direction) before eventually being blind. When last visited, Chapel Shaft was seen as an 'extruded' cylindrical plug of mud and rock, filling the height of the chamber, with water emerging in one corner. The floor at this point was then nearly dry, only carrying the water descending Chapel Shaft.

It should be appreciated that exploration to the depth of the 112 Yard Level (and the 90 Yard Level) is difficult and the number of persons who have been to these depths in the late 20th Century and since probably totals less than 20 and probably nobody has visited these areas on more than four occasions.

SCMC members on the 112 Yard Level, working their way towards the collapse near the bottom of Engine Shaft. *(Kelvin Lake - I.A.Recordings)*

Between Perkins Level and the 40 Yards Level

Surveys of the mine dating from the Snailbeach Company days do not show Perkins Level or any workings above the 40 Yard Level. It is presumed that all of these higher workings date from the Halvans Company days and later. In fact there are considerable workings above the 40 Yard Level.

In addition to the large chamber accessed via Perkins Level, there are other workings to the south-east that also continue down to the 40 Yard Level. These workings included a large stope open to surface but the upper part of these were in-filled during the reclamation works in the late 1990s. The lower parts of these workings remain open and parts of them are involved in the complex route normally used by current mine explorers to access the 40 Yard Level.

In recent years, mine explorers have extended their explorations to other parts of the upper workings and alternative routes to the 40 Yards Level have been established. These alternative routes are at times extremely exposed, skirting around the face of the vast open stope. While exploring the parallel workings and setting up these alternative routes, a number of other levels have been encountered that have been cut through by the upper parts of stope. Throughout these upper workings, occasional tools or other mine artefacts are regularly encountered.

SCOTT LEVEL (SJ37270210)

The portal is about 45ft below the mine datum (George's Shaft) and the level runs horizontally for about 1,400ft in a south-easterly direction. It averages 7ft wide and 7½ft high. For the first 165ft the roof and sides are stone lined and from then on in solid rock. Just into the solid rock section are the remains of a concrete dam. At 460ft there is a shaft, the top of which is capped with a bat grill and can be seen in the woods west of the Cornish engine house. The bottom 100ft of this shaft is filled with dirt and rubble, some of which has run into Scott Level partially blocking it. The top section of the shaft is still open and contains a cast iron 6 inch diameter water pipe. About 60ft from the surface the pipe turns through 90 degrees and enters a horizontal tunnel which comes out to the surface in gully on the side of the hill. When the level was converted for use as a water supply for the local community, it is thought that this pipe was used to pump the water out.

At 36ft past the shaft are the remains of the timber and brick dam. The level then joins a vein at a T-junction and, turning right in a south westerly direction, the workings can be followed for about 260ft if you don't mind being immersed up to the neck for a short distance! The other arm at the T junction heads north-east on the vein for 1,640ft. There is a water filled shaft in a short branch on the right, close to the T-junction, which has been plumbed to 115ft. The far end of Scott Level is estimated to be at a considerable depth below Yew Tree Level, which is located due south of Lords Hill chapel.

Remains of the first dam inside Scott Level. *(Kelvin Lake-I.A.Recordings)*

The large wooden plug from the second dam in Scott Level. *(Kelvin Lake-I.A.Recordings)*

Snailbeach District Railway

The joint Great Western Railway / London North Western Railway main line was extended from Hanwood Junction to Minsterley in 1861. This stimulated several plans for a railway from Pontesbury along the Hope Valley to serve passengers and the lead mines. In 1873 the Snailbeach District Railways Company was incorporated by Act of Parliament but, when it opened in 1877, it only served to take coal and supplies up to the mines and lead or lead ore back. It ran a distance of 3 miles at a gradient of 1 in 38 from sidings at Pontesbury to a terminus at Crowsnest, also known as Snailbeach Station. From here, a reverse branch ran, on a gradient of 1 in 25, to the Snailbeach Mine where the locomotive shed was built. There were plans to extend it to Tankerville Mine but this section was never built. The gradient meant that trains returning to Pontesbury could operate under gravity. This was a narrow gauge railway and the original Act of Parliament approving it specified that the gauge should be not less than 2'4".

At first the railway made a small profit, serving several of the lead mines in the area, but in 1884 the Tankerville, Pennerley and Bog Mines closed down, thus halving the line's traffic. From that time onwards, it continued with its main customer being the Snailbeach Mine and from 1892 it appears to have been run as part of the mining company. At the turn of the century, great efforts were made by Henry Dennis to revive the railway as a separate company but this was at a time when the price of lead was low and Snailbeach Mine was only just surviving. Dennis managed to keep it going, however, with the carriage of other material such as processed mine waste and roadstone. The opening in 1905 of a new roadstone quarry at Eastridge came at the right time and a branch was laid to it. This now became the main customer, although some traffic was still carried from Snailbeach Mine. A record 38,000 tons was carried in 1909 but this had fallen to 8,800 tons by 1912. When the Snailbeach Mine finally closed, the railway was

[36 & 37 Vict.] *The Snailbeach District Railways* [**Ch. ccxxxi.**]
Act, 1873.

CHAPTER ccxxxi.

An Act for making a railway from Pontesbury to Snailbeach and Tankerville in the county of Salop. [5th August 1873.] A.D. 1873.

WHEREAS the making of the railways herein-after described in the county of Salop will be of great public and local advantage:

And whereas the persons in this Act named, with others, are willing, at their own expense, to construct the railways, and are desirous to be incorporated for the purpose:

And whereas it is expedient that the Snailbeach Mine Company, Limited, should be authorised to subscribe towards the said undertaking:

And whereas plans and sections showing the lines and levels of the railways authorised by this Act, and also books of reference containing the names of the owners and lessees, or reputed owners and lessees, and of the occupiers of the lands required or which may be taken for the purposes or under the powers of this Act, were duly deposited with the clerk of the peace for the county of Salop, and are herein-after respectively referred to as the deposited plans, sections, and books of reference:

And whereas the purposes of this Act cannot be effected without the authority of Parliament:

May it therefore please Your Majesty that it may be enacted; and be it enacted by the Queen's most Excellent Majesty, by and with the advice and consent of the Lords Spiritual and Temporal, and Commons, in this present Parliament assembled, and by the authority of the same, as follows:

1. This Act may be cited as "The Snailbeach District Railways Act, 1873." Short title.

2. "The Railways Clauses Consolidation Act, 1845," "The Companies Clauses Consolidation Act, 1845," "The Lands Clauses Provisions of Acts herein named incorporated.

[*Local.—231.*]   A   1

"Fernhill" an 0-6-0ST loco, possibly built by Barclays & Co. Purchased by the SDR in 1881. The name was that of the residence of J.H.Lovett one of the SDR Directors at the time. Engine scrapped about 1906. *(K.C. Lock)*

Loco "No.2" about 1935. A Kerr Stuart 0-4-2T built in 1902, it was bought by Colonel Stephens for use on the SDR in 1922. *(K.C. Lock)*

One of the Baldwin 4-6-0PT locos hauling empty SDR wagons back to the mine over the Shrewsbury Road bridge, Pontesbury in 1940s. Built for the War Department in 1916/17 a pair of these engines were acquired by the SDR in 1923. Both were scrapped in 1950. *(K.C. Lock)*

Loco "No.2" about 1935, possibly in the sidings at Pontesbury. It worked on the line until 1946, finally being scrapped in 1950. *(K.C. Lock)*

In the 1930s SDR wagons were loaded with re-worked material from the mine spoil tips in a siding was just below the present day Village Hall car park. *(K.C. Lock)*

SDR Locos at the engine shed, Snailbeach in the 1920s. On the right is the remains of loco No.1 "Dennis" (scrapped in 1937) with No.2 in the doorway. Inside the shed on the left is one of the Baldwin locos, possibly loco No.4. *(Shropshire Mines Trust)*

unsuccessfully offered at a knock down price to the Marquis of Bath. Quarry traffic picked up, however, and the railway kept going though the First World War carrying barite and roadstone. When the Eastridge Quarry closed in 1921, traffic dropped off considerably and was less that 3,000 tons in 1922.

Closure was contemplated but a partnership consisting of a Colonel Stephens and several others took over the railway in 1923. Stephens had interests in several light railways around the country and it was almost a hobby. He replaced worn out sleepers with second-hand standard gauge sleepers cut in half and most of the rails with main line 45lbs rail. The Eastridge Quarry branch line was taken up. In 1877, the rolling stock consisted of 29 coal wagons, 12 hoppers, 6 timber wagons and 6 goods wagons. By 1924, this had been changed to 3 open wagons, 33 mineral wagons, 4 timber trucks and 1 'miscellaneous' vehicle. The change of type obviously demonstrated the change in traffic carried. The railway continued to function under Stephens, carrying barite from the mine plus processed mine tailings. In 1927, they had good luck once again when the Callow Hill Quarry opened and in 1928 they carried 4,821 tons of roadstone as well as mine traffic. Shropshire County Council took over the Callow Hill Quarry in 1930 and a siding was put in underneath a crushing plant. Crushed stone was loaded directly into wagons that would run to Pontesbury by gravity, where the County Council erected a tarring plant. There was steady traffic from Snailbeach and the quarry during the 1930s, although the trains only ran 3-4 times a week. It is believed that the railway was operated with only 1 driver-fitter, 1 platelayer, 1 junction man and 1 brakeman. Driver Gatford lived in a house next to the line and is rumoured to have often left his engine there overnight rather than return it to the locomotive shed!

By the mid-1940s, traffic from Snailbeach Mine had ceased and stone from the quarry had been reduced considerably, thus causing the railway to run at a loss. It was at this time that a legal dispute arose over the lease to the locomotive shed and its access. The railway had sub-let these from the Halvans

Company but, when the latter had ceased operations, the mine site had been taken over by Joe Roberts. At the end of 1944 he asked for an increased rent which the railway refused to pay as it was in the middle of a fixed lease. Roberts then cut off the water supply to the locomotive shed and removed 2 sections of rail. Although one locomotive was on the right side of this gap and could continue operations, two were trapped inside the shed. An injunction was applied for on the grounds that he was interfering with a statutory railway in wartime and he was made to replace the rails. The legal dispute carried on for nearly a year, however, and Roberts finally accepted that the SDR owned the rail track up to the engine shed. Both sides agreed a new 14 year lease of the locomotive shed itself, sidings and water supply and Roberts paid the railway £50 costs in lieu of compensation.

A new crisis arose when the boilers of all three locomotives were failed by a boiler inspector in 1946. As there were no funds to replace or repair these, an agricultural tractor was used to haul the empty trucks back to Callow Hill Quarry. There was sufficient space on either side of the track for a tractor to run with one pair of wheels between the tracks and the other outside. In 1947, Shropshire County Council leased the section of the line between Pontesbury and Callow Hill and operated it themselves using the tractor. The locomotives rusted away in the Locomotive Shed until they were cut up in 1950 and the rails between the Crows Nest terminus and Callow Hill were lifted shortly thereafter. The quarry then switched to road transport and by 1959 the last section of track fell out of use. The final lengths of rail were lifted in 1962, some being sold to the Talyllyn Railway, and the last wagons disposed of. The Snailbeach District Railway Company, however, remained in existence until it sold off its last asset, the track from Callow Hill Quarry to the road, in the 1970s. A few years ago, two of the Snailbeach wagons were found at Talyllyn Railway in very bad condition. These were recovered and the chassis of one can be seen in the Locomotive Shed. Another is being used as a base to be reconstructed.

Loco No.3 a 4-6-0PT Baldwin, built in 1916 for use by the War Department in France. Acquired by the SDR in January 1923. Scrapped 1950. *(K.C. Lock)*

Loco No.2 outside the engine shed, Snailbeach in the 1930s. *(Shropshire Mines Trust)*

A 1930s view of the Engine Shed at Snailbeach, with Loco No.4 (built in 1917 for the War Department) outside. In the background (right) is the New Crusher House, with it's roof almost intact. Other buildings on the dressing floor are also visible. *(Shropshire Mines Trust)*

Mr. J.Rowson and Mr. Edwards working a 'train' over the Shrewsbury Road bridge, Pontesbury in the 1950s. From 1947 to 1959 the Pontesbury to Callow Hill section was leased to Shropshire County Council who used the Fordson tractor to haul empty wagons up to the Callow Hill quarry. The steam locomotives were withdrawn from service in 1946. *(Emily Griffiths Collection)*

There were 6 different locomotives (the last 4 numbered 1-4) used on the railway at different times. These were :

Belmont : 0-4-2ST by Henry Hughes & Company. Built in 1874 for Ifton-Rhyn Colliery and acquired by SDR in 1877. Scrapped 1912.

Fernhill : 0-6-0ST by Barclay & Company. Acquired by SDR new in 1881. Scrapped 1906.

Dennis (No.1) : 0-6-0T by W G Bagnall Ltd. Acquired by SDR new in 1906. Scrapped 1937.

Skylark (No.2) : 0-4-2T by Kerr Stuart. Built in 1902 as a contractor's locomotive during building of the Leek & Manifold Light Railway and, after several other owners, acquired by SDR in 1923. Scrapped 1950.

Ex-War Dept (No.3) : 4-6-0PT by Baldwin. Built in 1916 for WD and acquired by SDR in 1923. Scrapped 1950.

Ex-War Dept (No.4) : 4-6-0PT by Baldwin. Built in 1917 for WD and acquired by SDR in 1923. Scrapped 1950.

The sidings at the rear of the Snailbeach engine shed onto the main dressing floor. *(I.A.Cooper)*

SDR enamelled notice warning trespassers to "Keep off".
(I.A.Cooper)

Wildlife

Vegetation

The Stiperstones ridge itself is mostly composed of quartzite, which gives rise to poor acidic soils and heathland. The underlying slopes are mainly Mytton Flags which give an acidic soil, often wet where springs emerge. Old mine tips are poor in nutrients and often toxic, with heavy metals and salts. The University of Liverpool carried out a study of tolerant species on waste tips at the nearby Bog Mine. They found that colonisation by plants is slow and usually follows a sequence of algae, then lichens, bryophytes and finally higher plant species such as Red Fescue, which shows a degree of lead tolerance. Eventually woody species such as heather, gorse and broom result in a heathy woodland vegetation dominated by birch. Many miners lived locally in isolated smallholdings, where they tried to grow vegetables to supplement their families' diet. Calcite was often added to the soil to try to neutralise the acidity as agricultural lime was expensive. Calcite is not as effective as lime but would have acted on the soil to some extent, explaining why small hay meadows can be found with their characteristic flora, eg greater butterfly orchid, mountain pansy and rough hawkbit.

Snailbeach is a rather interesting area to attempt to interpret. The calcite spoil heaps abandoned in the 1950s were not colonised with any vegetation and these were levelled off with topsoil by Shropshire County Council during the reclamation scheme. This lack of colonisation was due to a number of reasons, eg high levels of zinc which is phytotoxic, instability due to material acting as a sand dune and dry conditions due to the very porous conditions. The area of grassland just east of the car park was sown with a wildflower mix including chrysanthemum, corn marigold, cornflower, wild carrot and common knapweed. The mix also included poppy but this stopped flowering after a couple of years. To continue flowering, poppy requires the ground to be turned over in some way (hence why it was so common on 1st World War battlefields) so the seeds are probably dormant until the tips are disturbed again. Small species such as fairy flax are present around the mine workings and this may indicate richer soils there. One of the most surprising finds within the Snailbeach area is of large quantities of spurge laurel, false-brome and woodruff, which usually indicate the site of an ancient woodland.

Bats

In February 1993, the Shropshire Bat Group was invited to descend Sheep Shaft at Snailbeach into Perkins Level to establish the presence of bats. At that time, a consultant's report had recommended infilling most of the stopes but a significant population of bats was found in a large stope close to surface. Enough bats were found to be sure that this was an important site, which should be protected, leading to a visit by Bob Stebbings representing English Nature a few weeks later. They were mostly lesser horseshoe bats, which are quite scarce and threatened nationally, although they are the commonest bat in our local mines. They are near the northern limit of their range here, being confined to the southern and western parts of Britain. It was agreed to keep this stope open after all to preserve the bats' hibernation area and to allow access for explorers.

Female bats get together in summer and deliver and rear their young in communal roosts near to suitable feeding areas. lesser horseshoe bats, which are the most frequent and important kind found in Snailbeach Mine, like to breed in certain kinds of large old houses. Male bats live singly or in small groups. Both sexes of Lesser Horseshoes hibernate, either singly or in groups which may be mixed, in caves or mines that may be several miles from their summer feeding areas. Bats in the Snailbeach mines are probably associated with a known summer roost a few miles away in Shropshire, which is probably also used by the bats which hibernate at nearby Huglith mine. Lesser horseshoe and other bats also use the mines throughout the year.

Summer use is probably only by males, which are joined by females in the autumn for courtship, mating and then hibernation. Overall the numbers have been fairly constant over the years, with some indications of an increase recently (see table below). The numbers hibernating in any year must be affected by the fortunes of the local summer roosts. The counts at Snailbeach mine are certainly a substantial underestimate. They do not include the bats which are seen deeper in the mine during explorations by SCMC members. These tend to be widely scattered through the workings, only a small proportion of which are accessible to humans, but easily reached by bats. There must be many which we do not see. The counts at Huglith and Riddleswood, included for comparison, are also incomplete, but probably not to the same degree, while the New Central counts will be more or less comprehensive.

Counts of lesser horseshoe bats in local abandoned mines

	96	97	98	99	00	01	02	03	04	05
Perkins Level	11	19	19	21	19	24	23	26	41	36
New Central Mine	16	29	23	21		23	25	45	47	47
Huglith - Badger Level	8	13	4	13	19	21	15	8	25	25
Huglith - Riddleswood							41	62	63	79

A lesser horseshoe bat (Rhinolophus hipposideros) in a typical 'sleeping' pose. When hunting they use echo location to detect prey, which they can pick off branches and rocks. They mainly eat mosquitoes, craneflies, gnats, lacewings, moths, beetles and spiders. They are one of several varieties of bat that can be found in the Snailbeach mine workings. *(Shropshire Caving & Mining Club)*

Cave Animals

In February 2005 a survey was carried out to see what wildlife existed underground in the mine. There are 3 zones in any underground habitat, ie

- **Threshold** – within a few feet of the entrance with lots of light and subject to the same temperature changes as outside
- **Threshold Hypogean** – further in with the entrance still in sight but temperature is more stable
- **Dark Hypogean** – no light whatsoever and with a stable temperature. Unless a passage has a significant draught, the temperature remains the same throughout the year, thus being warm in winter and cool in summer. In the far reaches of Perkins Level, the temperature averages 8°C.

The types of small animal found underground can also be classified into 3 types, ie

- **Troglophiles** – animals that can live either on surface or underground and spend part of their lifecycle underground, eg bats or flies that hibernate underground in winter. This also includes spiders that live just inside entrances but can equally be found on surface.
- **Troglobites** – animals that spend all of their life underground in the dark. These are usually white and blind with long antennae as the lack of light means that there is no need for camouflage colouring or eyes.
- **Trogloxenes** – animals that can be found occasionally underground but cannot survive there for long. An 'accidental trogloxene' might be a worm that is carried into the mine by rainwater flowing through cracks, it will not live long. A 'habitual trogloxene' is an animal that

returns underground for short periods but does not live there, this includes human explorers!

Small cave animals avoid disturbance so it is extremely unlikely that you will ever see any, as even creeping along can sound like an earthquake to them – causing them to hide in inaccessible cracks. The only way is to lay traps containing a mixture of sugar, Guinness and black treacle that is boiled up and allowed to coagulate into a sticky gel. The smell is irresistible to them and they will climb onto the surface to feed and become stuck there. It is vital if you use these traps that you check them the following day and gently release the animals after identifying them. If not, you could remove the complete animal population of the mine in a very short time!

Caves tend to have a wider variety of animals than mines since they have been available as a habitat for millions of years, whereas mines could only be up to 100 years old At Snailbeach, we found a number of troglophiles close to the entrance of Day Level and Perkins Level. These obviously used this area to either shelter from cold weather or, in the case of spiders, to prey on such animals. The ones so far identified are :-

- Herald Moth
- Tissue Moth
- Gnats
- Spiders

Some nematode worms were found in Perkins Level next to a crack in the roof but these were most likely accidental trogloxenes carried in from the surface.

The only troglobites found were springtails called Folsomia fimetaria and these were only in Day Level. There is no guarantee that they do not exist in Perkins Level, they just were not found in the traps at that time.

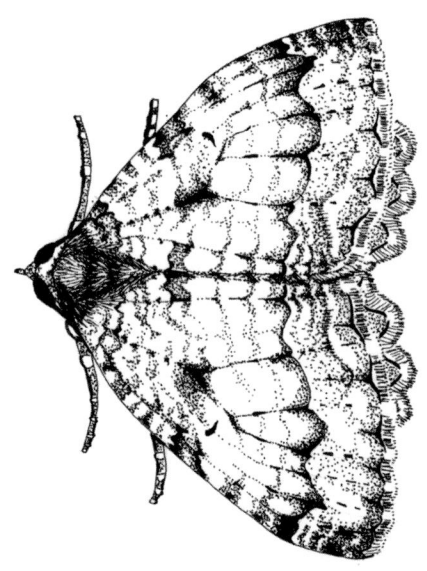

Triphosa dubitata (Tissue Moth) - has a slightly glossy purplish appearance. Its preferred habitats are woodland, heathland, chalk and limestone areas.

The adults fly in August and September. Many of them can be found overwintering in the adits at Snailbeach (often quite a long way inside), before reappearing in April and May. *(Pam Curley)*

Scoliopteryx libatrix (Herald Moth) - a very colourful noctuid moth (one which flies at night) that overwinters as an adult and can be found hibernating on the walls and roof of Day Level and Perkins Level. The species is fairly common throughout Britain. The larvae feed on willow and poplar. *(Kelvin Lake - I.A.Recordings)*

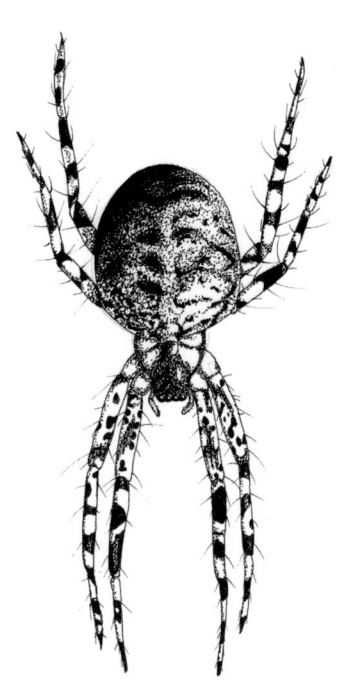

Meta merianae (Cave Spider) - a troglophile spider, it is an active predator and weaves circular cobwebs. Typically found inside the entrances of various adits around Snailbeach, such as Day Level or Perkins Level. *(Pam Curley)*

Meta merianae (Cave Spider) with water droplet on the metal sheeting inside the entrance to Perkins Level. *(Kelvin Lake - I.A.Recordings)*

Bibliography

Adams D R B	"Survey of the South Shropshire Lead Mining Area", 1962, SCMC Account No.2
Adams D R B	"Supplement to Account 2", 1968, SCMC Account 4
Bagshaw S	"History, Gazetteer and Directory of Shropshire 1851"
Brook F	"The Snailbeach Lead Mine, a Company History", 1976, SCMC Journal
Brook F & Allbutt M	"The Shropshire Lead Mines", 1973, Moorland Publishing
Brook F & Allbutt M	"The Snailbeach Lead Mine", 1969, Industrial Archaeology Society Journal No.2, Portsmouth College of Technology
Brook F & Allbutt M	"The Snailbeach Mining Company 1767-1911, 1969, Northern Cavern & Mines Research Society Memoirs
Brown IJ	"Mine Accidents in the South Shropshire Metalliferous Mining Area 1875-present", paper to University of Birmingham Dept of Extra-Mural Studies 1967-68
Brown IJ	"Notes on the Lead Smelt Houses of the South Shropshire Mining Area", 1980, SCMC Journal
Brown IJ	"Snailbeach Lead Mine near Minsterley, Shropshire", 1993, SCMC Account No.17

Brown IJ	"The Mines of Shropshire", 1976, Moorland Publishing
Brown IJ	"West Shropshire Mining Fields", 2001, Tempus Publications Ltd
Brown I & Heathcote J	"Plans & Sections of the Metalliferous Mines of SW Shropshire", 1972, SCMC Account No.10
Burt R et al	"The Mines of Shropshire & Montgomeryshire", 1990, University of Exeter Press
City of Hereford Archaeology Unit	"The Blacksmith's Shop, Snailbeach Mine, Shropshire", 1992
City of Hereford Archaeology Unit	"Tankerville Lead Mine, Pennerley, Shropshire", 1991
Cope Rev J	"The Snailbeach Disaster", privately published 1897
Corfield M	"There are People in Snailbeach with Vivid Memories of the Mine Disaster of 60 Years Ago", Shropshire Magazine April 1955
Davies TJ	"Engine Houses of the Mines of South Shropshire", privately published, 1969
Davies TJ	"Jones v The Snailbeach Mining Company 1897", 1979, SCMC Journal
Davies TJ, et al	"Mining Remains in South-West Shropshire", 1993, SCMC Account No.18

Davis RV	"A Brief Account of the Geology, History & Mechanisation of the Snailbeach Mine, Shropshire", 1969, Northern Cavern & Mines Research Society Memoirs
Dickinson H & Jenkins R	"James Watt and the Steam Engine", 1981, Oxford
Dines HG	"The West Shropshire Mining Region", 1958, Bulletin of the Geological Survey No.14
Fowler RP	"Geology of the Shelve Mining Region", 1994, SCMC Account No.21
Francis P et al	"Never on a Sunday", 2000, Shropshire Mines Trust
Gaydon A	"Victoria County History of Shropshire", 1968, Vol. viii
Geological Survey	"Barium Minerals in England & Wales", 1945, HMSO
Geological Survey	"Barytes & Witherite", 1922, Geological Survey Special Report Vol. II
Geological Survey	"Special Report on the Mineral Resources of Great Britain - Barytes & Witherite", 1916, HMSO
Geological Survey Hair P	"Wartime Pamphlet No.46", 1945, Geological Survey "Industrial and Domestic Violence in Shropshire in the 1820s", 1983, Transactions of the Shropshire Archaeological Society No.64

Hall T	"Report on the Shropshire Mining District", 1919, privately printed
Haszard R	"The Metalliferous Mining Area of Shropshire", 1964, Proceedings British Speleological Association No.2
Heathcote J	"Survey of the Metal Mines of South West Shropshire", 1979, SCMC Account No.12
HMSO	"The King's Works in Wales 1277-1330"
Holding S R	"Snailbeach Recent Exploration", 1992, SCMC Account No.15
Holding S R	"Recent Changes at Snailbeach", 1993, SCMC Journal
Holding S et al	"A Survey of the Metal Mines of South Shropshire", 1993, Supplement to SCMC Account No.12
Janes B	"The Snailbeach District Railways", 2005, The Colonel Stephens Museum website hfstephens-museum.org.uk
Liscombe & Co	"The Mines of Cardiganshire, Montgomeryshire & Shropshire", 1989, S Hughes Mining Services
Machin R	"Short List of the Depths worked in the Lead Mines of Shropshire", 1985, Newsletter of the Hereford Caving Club, 39, p.23
Merry D	"The History of Minsterley". 1976, privately printed

Moissenet M	"Annales des Mines", 1862, Paris
Moissenet M	"Lead Mining & Smelting in the Snailbeach District", 1862, Mining & Smelting Magazine
Morriss R Morton G	"The Powder Magazine, Snailbeach Mine", Report "Geology of the Shelve Mining District", 1869
Murchison RI	"The Silurian System", 1839, London
Newton M	"Crumbling Walls, Rusting Tramways, Shapeless Masses of Shale", Shropshire Magazine July 1972
Newton M	"Requiem for a Railway, born 1877, died 1946", Shropshire Magazine October 1977
Newton M	"Rot & Ruin", Shropshire Magazine April 1963
Newton M	"Snailbeach – Shropshire's Greatest Lead Mine", Shropshire Magazine October 1978
Newton M	"The Colonel's Little Railway", Shropshire Magazine, September 1985
Newton M	"The Mines at Snailbeach – Eyesores or Reminders of a Vital Past?" Shropshire Magazine February 1972
Pearce AJ	"Metalliferous Mines of Shropshire, Volume 1 - Gazetteer", 1994, SCMC Account No.20
Pearce AJ	"Metal Mines of Shropshire", 1997, SCMC Account No.22

Pearce AJ	"Pre-Roman mining in Shropshire", 1991, Shropshire Caving and Mining Club Journal, pp.5-6.
Pearce AJ et al	"Mining in Shropshire", 1995, Shropshire Books
Read H H	"Rutley's Mineralogy 25th Edition", 1962, Thomas Murby & Company
Robinson A	"Technical Aspects of Snailbeach Phase 1", 1993, SCMC Journal
Southwick S & Brueton S	"Excavation of the Mine Managers Office at Snailbeach Mine", 1997, SCMC Journal
Smith B	"Memoirs of the Geological Survey Vol XX111", 1922, HMSO
Smith B & Dewey H	"Special Reports on the Mineral Resources of Great Britain, Vol.23, Lead and Zinc Ores in the Pre-Carboniferous Rocks of West Shropshire and North Wales", 1922, Geological Survey
Toghill P	"Geology in Shropshire", 1990, Swan Hill
Tonks ES	"The Snailbeach District Railways", 1974, Industrial Railway Society
Turner E	"Lead Mining in Shropshire", 1943, Transactions of the Caradoc & Severn Valley Field Club No.12
Tylecote RF	"The Prehistory of Metallurgy in the British Isles", 1990, Transactions Institute of Metallurgy 46

Wadlow EC	"Shropshire was an Important Lead Producing Area a Century Ago", Shropshire Magazine, April 1959
Wadlow EC	"The Story of Shropshire's Lead Industry", The Metal Industry 27/7/34
Whild S	"The Vegetation of the Stiperstones Mines", 2002, Shropshire Botanical Society Newsletter 6

Birmingham City Library - Boulton & Watt Collection

Gentleman's Magazine, 1786, pages 924-5.

Illustrated London News, 4th October 1856

Mining & Smelting Magazine, 1862

Mining Journal, 1840-1880

Notes from lectures on the Shropshire mines held at Pontesbury in 1966

Public Record Office - Pipe Rolls of Henry II, 1179-1184

Reports of HM Mines Inspectorate

Shropshire Archives - Longueville Collection, plans, etc.

Shropshire Caving & Mining Club Library

Shropshire Magazine

Transactions of the Caradoc & Severn Valley Field Club

Wellington Journal, 1874-1900

Wiltshire & Swindon Record Office - Longleat Papers

Glossary of Terms

ACCOUNT MEN	Miners paid at a daily rate.
ADIT	Horizontal tunnel into a mine.
ADVENTURERS	Shareholders in a mine.
ATTLE	Rubbish or deads from the mine.
BACK	Part of the vein nearest the surface.
BALANCE BOX	A counter weight attached to the pump rod of an engine to assist in raising it.
BARGAIN	Agreement between mine agent and mining team to mine ore for a set price for a month.
BARITE	Barium Sulphate - used in the manufacture of paint and paper.
BEAT AWAY	To drive a level.
BED	Horizontal .
BELLAND	Powdered lead ore, which can poison water courses and pasture.
BING	Large lumps of lead ore requiring little dressing.
BLACK JACK	Zinc Sulphide (also called Sphalerite or Blende).
BOB	The beam of a steam engine or balance box.
BORER	Drill rod for hand drilling.
BUCKING IRON	Flat faced hammer for crushing lead ore.
BUDDLE	Wooden frame or other device over which a flow of water passes to separate lead ore from waste.
BURROW	Dumps or tailings from the mine.

CAPTAIN	Experienced mine manager.
CATHEAD	Small capstan winch.
CHARGER	Copper or bronze rod with an open trough at one end used to place gunpowder into a horizontal shothole.
CLACK	A pump valve.
COBBING	Breaking down the ore to separate it from waste rock.
COFFIN LEVEL	Old level driven without explosive that is wider at shoulder level, hence the name from its shape.
COUNTRY ROCK	The strata through which the vein passes.
CROSS CUT	A level driven at right angles to the vein for access.
DAMP	Gas.
DEADS	Waste rock, often stacked underground.
DIAL	Miner's surveying compass.
DRIFT	See ADIT.
EGG & EYE	The notch and slot made in opposite sides of a shaft or level for a wooden prop or support.
ELVE	Handle of a pick.
ENGINE SHAFT	Shaft where the pumps operate.
FATHOM	Unit of measurement - 6 feet.
FAULT	Dislocation of strata (beds) caused by earth movements.
FLAT RODS	Horizontal beams for transmitting motion from an engine or waterwheel to a shaft some distance away.
FORK	A mine is "in fork" when the engine can cope with pumping out the water.

FLUKE	Head of a charging rod.
FUSE	Straw or quill filled with fine gunpowder that burns slowly to allow time for miner to escape before it sets off the charge.
GAD	Iron wedge for splitting rock.
GATE	Large passage underground.
GIN	Engine.
GRASS	Surface of a mine.
HADE	Inclination of the vein.
HALVANS	Ore bearing rock not considered worthy of recovery.
HANGING WALL	Wall or side overhanging the lode.
HUSH	Narrow valley eroded by damming water and releasing it to carry away topsoil, thus exposing lead veins.
HUTCH	Box for carrying ore.
JAGGER	Packhorse driver.
JIGGER	Mechanical sieve for separating ore.
KNOCKINGS	Lead ore with spar as cut from the vein.
KIBBLE	Barrel-shaped iron bucket for raising ore.
LANDER	Person who unloads kibble or cage at shaft top.
LAUNDER	Wooden trough for directing flow of water.
LETTING	Auction where mine manager would offer areas of the mine to be worked by the team charging the least price for lead ore produced.
LEVEL	Horizontal tunnel.
LODE	Ore deposit.

LEAT	Surface water course.
MAD WATER	Water that quickly returns back into the mine from which it has just been pumped.
MUNDIC	Iron pyrites (fool's gold)
OFFAL	Waste rock including irrecoverable ore.
OLD MAN	Miners' term for previous miner or ancient mine workings.
ORE	Mineral that was mined.
PARCEL	Heap of dressed ore ready for sale.
PIECEWORK	Method of working whereby there would be an agreed price for a certain bit of work.
PITMAN	Miner responsible for maintenance of pitwork.
PITWORK	Pump pipes, pumps, etc in a shaft.
PRICKER	Thin pointed rod made of copper or bronze used to put a hole through wadding in a shot hole for the fuse to fit.
POINT OF HORSE	Place where the lode divides into one or more branches.
PUNCH	Timber support.
RISE	Underground shaft driven upwards.
RIDER	Rock dividing a lode.
SETT	Leased area of a mine.
SHAFT	Vertical entrance to a mine.
SHEARS	Wooden headgear over a shaft.
SMITHAM	Powdered lead ore.
SOLE	Lowest part of a mine or level.
SOUGH	Drainage level.
SUMP	Underground shaft driven downwards.

STOPE	Worked out vein, left as an open cavity.
STRIKE	Course of a vein.
STULL	Timber support, sometimes used to make a platform on which deads are placed.
TAMPER	Rod with a copper or bronze end used to compress gunpowder in a shothole.
TAILINGS	Waste material from ore washing process.
TROUBLES	Faults or interruptions in the lode.
TUBBING	Iron or timber rings in a shaft to support brickwork.
TUTWORK	Method of working where payment was made for driving shafts or levels at a set price per fathom.
UNDERLIE SHAFT	Shaft sunk on the course of a lode.
VEIN	Vertical or near-vertical deposit of ore, often in a fault.
WADDING	Clay placed in the end of a shothole after gunpowder has been inserted to direct the blast into the rock.
WHIM	Winding engine, either horse or steam powered.
WINDER	Steam engine used for winding in a shaft.
WINDLASS	Hand operated winch for pulling loads up a shaft.
WINZE	Underground shaft driven downwards.
WASTES	Areas where ore has been extracted and the cavity filled with deads.

Shropshire Mines Trust Ltd

The Trust is a charity that was set up in March 1996 and incorporated in 2005. Our members are made up of mining historians and other local people with an interest in their mining remains. Mining used to be one of the major industries of Shropshire and it lasted from the Roman period up to the mid-20th Century. All of this activity left spoil heaps, buildings and other structures throughout the county. Up until 1960, many of the surface structures still remained from mines which had been closed half a century earlier but now most of these have been lost forever.

Strangely, as the remains get less the public interest in industrial archaeology seems to be growing and over the past few years there has been great demand to see the working conditions of our ancestors. This is reflected at Ironbridge Gorge Museum and Snailbeach Mine where the County Council has preserved the unique surface remains. There is no cause for complacency, however, as there are engine houses at other mines in Shropshire, which are almost complete but in imminent danger of collapse. There are also many other sites with lesser remains that still deserve some form of preservation. Unless something is done over the next few years, our children in future will have to rely on photographs and descriptions in books.

The first major project of the Trust was at the Tankerville Lead Mine near Shelve. The landowner generously donated the mine site to the Trust and, thanks to Shropshire County Council, South Shropshire District Council and English Heritage, work has been done to cap the shaft and repair the engine house and other surface features. The site is open for the public to walk around.

The Trust has assisted Shropshire County Council with preservation at Snailbeach Mine and has now taken over management of the site and the responsibility for showing visitors around. There is still much to do on site to make it more meaningful for visitors and any help is gratefully accepted.

Other activities the Trust is involved with include :-

- Display of artefacts at shows, etc
- Creation of mining trails
- Preserving other mining features
- Erecting memorials to the miners
- Recording memories of miners' families.

The Trust is acquiring a major collection of mining tools, machines and other equipment representing metalliferous and coal mining. These are being sited in appropriate places within and outside the county. We have also put together a mobile display thanks to T O Tomlins Ltd, which we take to steam rallies and other events. The Trust website is shown below where you will find the up to date contact details.

http://shropshiremines.org.uk/

Trust member issuing helmets and lights for visitors to Day Level *(A.J. Pearce)*

Shropshire Caving & Mining Club

The Club was formed as the Shropshire Mining Club in Newport on 6th September 1961 by a group of people interested in the exploration and study of disused mines in the County of Shropshire. It later changed its name to reflect its interest in natural caves as well. The Club has an active programme of underground trips, with about 3 main trips per month, including other parts of Britain, the Isle of Man, Ireland, and the Continent. The Club is a major force in the Midlands Cave Rescue Organisation, regularly participating in rescue practices and training.

Members also carry out historical research, the results of which the Club publishes either in:-

- Below (Quarterly Newsletter)
- Journal
- Accounts (occasional publications on specific topics or sites)
- Videos (produced in association with I.A.Recordings)

Members are also active in the preservation and conservation of underground and surface sites, working with other local groups and councils to protect bat habitats and sites of historical importance. Everybody has to start sometime and the Club organises training sessions and special trips to allow novices to learn the necessary skills without pressure. We use **S**ingle **R**ope **T**echniques (abseiling and prussiking) a great deal and experienced Club members are always willing to teach these skills and advise on the necessary personal equipment. The Club website is shown below where you will find the up to date contact details

http://www.serve.com/scmc/